3D BUSINESS ANALYST

Mohamed Elgendy

outskirts
press

Outskirts Press, Inc.
http://www.outskirtspress.com

ISBN: 978-1-4787-2640-1

Outskirts Press and the "OP" logo are trademarks belonging to Outskirts Press, Inc.

Dedication

*T*his book is dedicated to the two most important people in my life, my Mom and Dad. To my Mom, Dr. Huda Helayl, who dedicated her life raising me with the highest of morals and virtues. While being my source of spiritual guidance she was able to walk me through life's essential elements of success; organization, hard work, and never settling for less. My Dad, Dr. Ali Elgendy, is my lifetime mentor in both life and business. He remains as my source of inspiration, his words being "With hard work and good intentions, there is nothing you cannot achieve". His constant commitment to education and high work ethics continue to inspire me for a goal-driven and successful life. I believe it is my greatest fortune to have such great parents who continue to enrich every aspect of my life.

An exceptional thank you goes to my brother and best friend, Dr. Abdelrahman Elgendy. Through his adventurous soul I learned that success belongs to those who persevere long enough. His invaluable motivation and encouragement played a crucial role in writing this book.

And last but not least; my two beautiful sisters, Reham and Alaa Egendy, for always being there for me whenever I needed them.

Without my family, this project would have never become a reality. For that, and much more, I am most grateful!

Acknowledgements

A special gratitude goes to:

- Thom Kriner, Business Analysis Manager at Independence Blue Cross, for his sincere support and invaluable insight into this book. I can fairly say that Thom's encouragement and enthusiasm were the key elements driving me to write this book into completion.

- My editor, Heidi Enright, Project Manager at LiquidHub. Being one of the most effective people I came across, I truly believe any author aspiring for perfection will be lucky to have her expertise in his or her book.

- Katherine Markham, Program Manager at A2C, for the benefit of her rich experience in program & project management.

- Dot Byrne, Project Manager at Independence Blue Cross.

- My friend, Dr. Mahmoud Gaballa, for proofreading this book.

- Independence Blue Cross's business analysis team.

- Amerigroup's business analysis team.

- Cairo University, Cairo, Egypt.

- Nova Southeastern University, Florida, USA.

- Drexel University, Pennsylvania, USA.

- Smita Todkar and Sulekha Banerjee from iTechUS LLC.

- Colleen DiFabio and Mary Beth Ambros from Magic Hat Consulting.

- Karim Gaber from System Soft Technologies.

Contents

Dedication   iii

Acknowledgement   iv

Chapter 1 - Introduction   ix

Business Analysis   3

Roles and responsibilities of a BA   4

3D Business Analyst   7

Importance of the BA role   9

Skills and requirements for a good BA   9

Why become a Business Analyst?   10

Who should read this book?   11

Chapter 2 - Project Management for a Business Analyst   13

Project Management for a BA   15

Project Management Concepts   15

Project Management Knowledge Areas   25

The life of a project   26

Intersecting activities between the BA and PM   29

     Develop project charter   29

     Identifying stakeholders   30

     Project Scope Management   31

     Project Time Management   34

     Project Risk Management   37

     Perform change management   44

     Close project or phase   46

Chapter 3 - Requirements Management & Communication   51

I. Requirements Management   53

1. Elicit requirements   54

     Requirements elicitation techniques   55

     Where do we find requirements?   57

     Requirements Elicitation Tips   58

2. Analyze Requirements   59

     Define assumptions, dependencies and constraints   59

     Types of requirements   64

Categorizing requirements   64

Prioritizing requirements   69

Verify requirements (What are Good Requirements?)   69

Root-Cause Analysis   70

Fishbone diagram   70

5 Whys technique   71

3. Document and Present Requirements   73

Requirements Management Plan (RMP)   73

Requirements Traceability Matrix   74

Business Requirements Document (BRD)   75

User Stories   76

II. Requirements Communication   78

Chapter 4 - SDLC Methodologies   **85**

Software Development Life Cycle (SDLC)   87

Waterfall Methodology   93

Rational Unified Process (RUP)   95

Spiral Methodology   99

Prototyping   101

Rapid Application Development (RAD)   101

Agile Software Development   102

Scrum Methodology   103

Chapter 5 - Business Process Modeling   **113**

Unified Modeling Language (UML)   115

Types of UML Diagrams   116

1. Class Diagram   117

2. Component Diagram   118

3. Deployment Diagram   118

4. Package Diagram (Decomposition)   118

5. Statechart Diagram (State Machine Diagram)   119

6. Object Diagram   119

7. Sequence Diagram   120

8. Activity Diagram   122

9. Use Case Diagram   128

Tools to create UML Diagrams	138
Chapter 6 - Introduction to SQL	**141**
Structured Query Language (SQL)	143
1. Retrieve Data	145
2. SQL Data Manipulation Language (DML)	150
3. SQL Data Definition Language (DDL)	153
4. Querying More Than One Table	155
I. JOINS	155
II. UNION	157
III. INTERSECT	159
IV. Minus	160
Chapter 7 - Introduction to Lean Six Sigma	**167**
I. Lean Six Sigma	169
What is Waste (*Muda*)?	170
Principles of Lean Process:	170
1. Define Value	171
2. Identify Value Stream	173
3. Flow (make the process flow)	176
4. Pull	177
5. Seek Perfection	179
II. Six Sigma (6σ)	181
1. Define (customer & goals to understand problem)	182
2. Measure (where are we now?)	184
3. Analyze (understand why problems occur)	184
4. Improve (Solve problems)	185
5. Control (sustain achievements)	187
III. Integration	191
Chapter 8 - Templates	**197**
Project Charter	199
Work Breakdown Structure (WBS)	201
Change Management Plan	202
Change Request (CR)	203
Project Scope Statement	204

Risk Management Plan   205

Risk Register   208

Stakeholder Analysis Matrix   209

Stakeholders Management Strategy   210

Stakeholder Register   211

Business Requirements Document (BRD)   212

Inspection Checklist for Software Requirements   225

Requirement Traceability Matrix (RTM)   226

Use Case   228

Impact Assessment   233

Meeting Minutes   234

Attendance Sheet   235

RACI Matrix   236

Gap Analysis   237

REFERENCES   **239**

1

Introduction

Business Analysis

Business Analysis is the discipline of identifying the business needs and determining solutions to business problems. Solutions often include a system development component, but may also consist of process improvement, organizational change, strategic planning or policy development. The person who carries out this task is called a Business Analyst or BA.

The role of the Business Analyst is to work with the Business and IT Teams in developing technology solutions. The International Institute of Business Analysis (IIBA) defines the role as follows:

> *There is always a business need, our job is to clearly identify, analyze and document this need.*

"A business analyst works as a liaison among stakeholders in order to elicit, analyze, communicate, and validate requirements for changes to business processes, policies and information systems. The business analyst understands business problems and opportunities in the context of the requirements and recommends solutions that enable the organization to achieve its goals."

In other words, the Business Analyst acts as a bridge between business Subject Matter Experts (SME's) who have a business problem or opportunity and technology people who know how to create solutions for business process improvement. You might want to think of the business analyst as a translator who speaks several languages and without the BA, different team members will not be able to communicate with each other. Therefore, the BA is a person who can speak to the users, business people, development team, testers and architects each with their own language to bridge the gap between all stakeholders. (Figure 1-1)

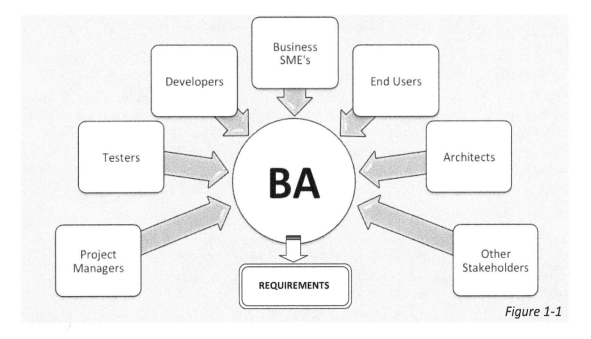

Figure 1-1

Roles and responsibilities of a BA

The primary role of the BA is to act as a liaison between the various stakeholders involved in a project. Defining all of the stakeholders and identifying their needs is the core of the business analyst role.

A structured business analysis role consists of the processes shown in figure 1-2:

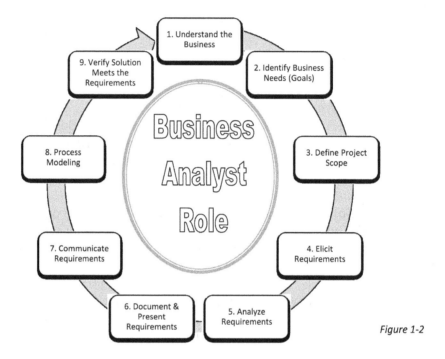

Figure 1-2

1. Understand the business

This is the first step in delivering a solution to a business problem or opportunity. It involves studying the product or service provided by the organization. The business analyst needs to understand the market that the business is trying to supply its products to. To do this, he or she has to identify the target customers for the products and services of the business (identifying the customers will be thoroughly explained in chapter 7).

2. Identify the business needs

The business needs are the goals and objectives of the project or the solution. In this process the BA communicates with the customers and end users – identified in the previous process – to gather their needs and understand why they want this project. This process is also called creating the Business Case (chapter 2).

3. Define the project scope

Before the BA can begin to elicit the actual requirements, he or she needs to ensure that the high level scope of the project is clear and complete. A complete project scope will describe all the parties that are involved with the project. This includes people, team members, systems, internal departments, vendors and customers. It should also include a high-level description of the project goals, risks, budget, schedule, assumptions, and business processes that will be covered as part of the solution, as well as a list of items that will not be included (chapter 2).

4. Elicit requirements:

This process is the main role of a business analyst. It is absolutely critical that the BA elicits the business requirements accurately to define a software solution. Eliciting requirements is an iterative process (chapter 3).

Some of the techniques that the BA can use are:
- Interviews with stakeholders
- Facilitated information gathering sessions
- Surveys and questionnaires
- Observation of stakeholders performing their tasks
- Study of existing systems and documentation

"60%-80% of project failures can be attributed directly to poor requirements gathering, analysis and management"
(Meta Group)

5. Analyze requirements

After requirements are gathered, they need to be prioritized, organized, specified, verified and validated using an iterative approach. As each requirement is analyzed, it generally leads to further questions. This requires the analyst to probe further until all relevant issues are cleared (chapter 3).

6. Document and present requirements

Now that the requirements have been obtained and analyzed, the BA has to document this data in a standard and consistent manner that is easily and clearly understood by all stakeholders. The information is then presented to the business SME's for review and signoff. Requirements can be documented and presented in many formats (chapter 3), such as:
- Requirements Management Plan
- Business Requirements Documents
- Process Flows
- Use Cases
- Graphs
- PowerPoint presentations
- Etc.

It is important that the information is presented to the business and technical audiences in a manner that is most appropriate for their understanding.

7. Communicate requirements

Once the requirements are clearly elicited, analyzed, documented and approved, they need to be communicated effectively to the concerned stakeholders. Requirements communication is an important skill for a 3D Business Analyst, where he/she will be working to bring different stakeholders and implementers of the project to a common understanding of the requirements and to get their buy-in on the final solution. This is done by conducting a series of interviews, meetings, workshops and JAD sessions that include all the relevant team members when communicating requirements to ensure that everyone understands the issues involved in the same way and to clarify any misunderstandings and unclear requirements (chapter 3).

> *"Poorly defined applications (miscommunication between business and IT) contribute to 66% project failure rate, costing U.S. businesses at least $30 billion every year"*
> *(Forrester Research)*

To understand how to effectively communicate with stakeholders, you need to be familiar with the communication concepts below:
- Communication plan
- Communication model
- Effective communication
- Efficient communication
- Communication method
- Communication types

8. Process Modeling

It is creating diagrammatic process flows of the system in both the current (As-Is) and future (To-be) states that can be used at any stage of the software development life cycle (SDLC) to visualize and document the system artifacts. Process modeling promotes better understanding of the requirements and it is a very effective way of communicating with stakeholders (customers, domain experts, designers, developers, etc.).

There are various types of UML diagrams that the BA creates in a project, such as:
- Use case diagrams
- Sequence diagrams
- Activity diagrams

These will be explained in detail in chapter 5.

9. Verifying that the solution meets the requirements

After the project handoff to the technical team, the business analyst continues to remain involved in order to ensure that the technical design meets business requirements and usability standards, the developed software meets the project goals, and the final product passes quality assurance tests and user acceptance.

It is obvious from the above that business analysis plays a crucial role in the success of any project from the start to the finish. The BA's role is very important in every stage of the system development life cycle (SDLC), explained in chapter 4, and in ensuring that the solution produced meets the business goals of all the stakeholders involved.

3D Business Analyst

Now that you understand what business analysis is, who the business analyst is and the roles and responsibilities of a BA, it is time to get introduced to the new term in Business Analysis: The 3D Business Analyst.

The 3D Business Analyst is the person who has strong project management and lean six sigma skill sets in addition to his or her BA expertise. Since the business analysis products are utilized by analysts, project managers, developers, testers, IT Architects, and other professionals working on improving the business process and IT applications, the need for a business analyst who is knowledgeable of these areas has arisen. This unique blend of the three distinct specialties provides the BA with the necessary concepts, theories, terminologies that allow him or her to communicate with stakeholders using their specific language and realize their expectations. Therefore, adding the two dimensions of project management and lean six sigma to the BA skill set helps the BA communicate with stakeholders more effectively and deliver his/her products more efficiently.

Let's see what the skill sets of 3D Business Analyst are:

First Dimentsion: Business Analysis
The 3D Business Analyst shall be proficient in the following business analysis knowledge areas:
- Requirements Management - elicit, analyze and document (Chapter 3)
- Requirements Communication (Chapter 3)
- SDLC Methodologies (Chapter 4)
- Process Modeling (Chapter 5)
- SQL (Chapter 6)

Second Dimension: Project Management (Chapter 2)
The project management knowledge area allows the BA to see the big picture of the project and understand how it fits within the organization.

The two worlds of project management and business analysis overlap in many areas. This is why project management became a mandatory skill for a sucessful BA.

In this book you will learn the basic concepts of project management and the different terminologies used by project managers. This will give you the opportunity to understand the different types of organizations, types of projects, team members' roles, project phases and knowledge areas as defined by the Project Management Institute (PMI).

Third Dimension: Lean Six Sigma (Chapter 7)
The Lean Six Sigma dimension adds depth to the BA's knowledge. Much of the business analysis work is about improving the process implemented by considering a problem, finding the root cause(s), developing alternative solutions and recommending the best solution for the situation.

In this book you will be introduced to the process improvement world. You will learn the power of Lean Six Sigma, the lean principles, the five phases of the DMAIC process, and understand the basic Lean Six Sigma tool set.

The more skill, experience and "thinking tools" available to an analyst, the more likely they will ask the right questions and produce high quality requirements artifacts.

As a 3D Business Analyst, you are empowered to:
- Ask the right questions to understand the process before committing to a solution
- Ask more questions until you reach the root cause
- Communicate effectively and efficiently
- Apply new techniques, methods, and processes to perform your job
- Suggest new approaches of executing business processes in the organization
- Analyze instead of accept
- See the big picture to add value to the organization as a whole
- Define and solve business problems

> **3D Business Analysis is a unique blend of three distinct specialties – business analysis (BA), project management (PM) and lean six sigma (LSS) with traditionally separate skill sets and career paths. However, when the components of these skill sets are analyzed and understood, a clear overlap emerges, and if used together, they provide the BA with the necessary concepts, theories and terminologies to allow him or her to communicate more effectively with stakeholders using their specific language, realize expectations and add more value to the organization.**

Importance of the BA role

By employing and empowering highly skilled business analysts, an organization will experience the benefit of improved relationships between IT and business areas.

Business managers tend to call business analysts for advice and counsel when considering an initiative that may involve computer technology. They generally find it easier to communicate with the business analyst than the technologist. In their role as a filter, the business analyst helps the business manager determine whether the initiative is practical and feasible and perhaps offer alternative ways of solving the problem.

Want to know the value of the business analyst? Compute the time and money saved when the business analyst solves a problem or answers a question so that the IT project does not have to be executed. Compute the time saved when the business analyst can provide a quick answer or do the research to get the answer instead of the business person taking time away from production to do it. The result of this calculation gives you an idea of the value of a business analyst.

Skills and requirements for a good BA

The good news is, a skilled business analyst does not need to have an IT background or deep technology knowledge. One of the most critical skills for success in this role is the ability to translate a business requirement or function into terms that are meaningful to software developers.

The typical skills of a good business analyst include:
- Interviewing skills – Business analysts spend their time communicating, asking questions and conveying needs
- Communication skills – Business analyst must be able to fully articulate requirements to the technical team before solutions are defined and implemented
- Facilitation skills – Business analysts spend most of their time facilitating elicitation sessions and helping the business and technical teams find solutions
- Documenting skills – Strong writing skills
- Analytical skills – Business analysts shall be detail-oriented, take time to understand

each problem and reach the root cause
- Project management skills – covered in chapter 2

 Why do you consider yourself a good BA? What are your strengths as a BA?

It is not hard to get hired, but what you should be looking for is to stand out from the rest of the crowd. That should be your goal. ALWAYS SEEK PERFECTION.

PERFECTION CARD

1. Be precise (direct and to the point)
2. Build up your reputation
3. Have a comprehensive plan and share it with your team
4. Stick to your deadlines – NEVER deliver late and do NOT deliver too early
5. Prepare for your meetings and ALWAYS be 2 minutes early
6. Even though our job is to ask questions, too many questions will not give your team the chance to discuss and come up with solutions
7. While being flexible is good, know your role and deliverables and don't get dragged into some secondary tasks
8. Know your team members roles – that will help you understand their expectations from you
9. Do not complain, get things done instead!!

Why become a Business Analyst?

- **Canadian employers will need 171,000 business analysis related professionals by 2016**
- (Source: Information and Communications Technology Council, 2011)
- **American employers will need 876,000 business analysis related professionals by 2020**
- (Source: U.S. Bureau of Labor Statistics, Employment Projections Program)
- BA jobs are increasing in this present market and economy about 36%
- Research shows the IT Analyst job to be the 7th best job in America
- BA is one of the top ten recession proof jobs, according to Forbes Magazine, and is top paid among the 10

- PayScale.com's list of America's best jobs for 2009 ranks business analyst among the top 10 high-growth job, with a massive 29% increase over the next ten years
- According to the U.S. Department of Labor and an IIBA salary survey, business analysts can earn from $60,000 to $130,000 per year

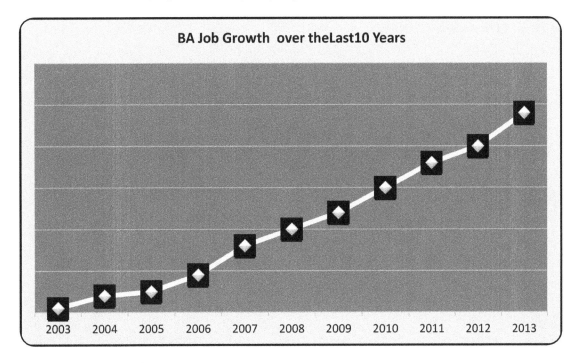

Who should read this book?

The initial idea of writing this book was to help fellow business analysts elevate their BA role to a 3D Business Analysis and fill any knowledge gaps. The project evolved to incorporate people who have decided to pursue a business analysis career path and would like some help making the transition.

This book offers a thorough explanation of the fundamentals of business analysis demonstrated by real time project examples, tips, situations and templates. Furthermore, it goes beyond that to a 3D business analysis by integrating the BA knowledge with project management skills and lean six sigma tools.

If you are a recent grad, non-IT professional or someone who already works in IT projects, the purpose of this book is to help you land a business analyst position. It will help you accumulate the knowledge, skills, methodologies and experience required to prepare for interviews and qualify yourself for a business analyst position.

If you are a business analyst, this book will guide you to take your role to another level. Being a 3D

Business Analyst means that you have opened new career horizons and you can start exploring a career in project management and business process improvement.

Once you accept a BA job, you can use this book as a hands-on reference guide for your day-to-day tasks. You don't need to read it from cover to cover; rather, keep it by your side as you work and refer to the relevant section as needed.

2

Project Management for a Business Analyst

Project Management for a BA

The two worlds of project management and business analysis overlap in many areas. This is why project management became a mandatory skill for a successful business analyst. In your day to day tasks as a BA you will be working side by side with the project manager in many activities throughout the project phases, starting from the initiation phase where the charter is created to identify the project goals moving through collecting requirements and defining the scope until the implementation and testing phases ending with the close phase and customer acceptance to the product.

In this chapter you will learn the basic concepts of project management and the different terminologies used by project managers. You will also be exposed to the project management knowledge areas as defined by the PMI (Project Management Institute) and the different organization structures. This will help you see the big picture of the project that you will be working on and how it fits within the organization.

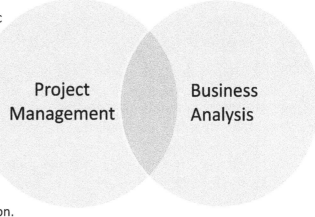

Figure 2-1

Project Management Concepts

Project vs. Program vs. Portfolio

Most work being done in organizations can be described as either operational (ongoing process) or project (temporary) work.

A Project

- Is a temporary endeavour with a beginning and an end
- Create a unique product, service, or result
- Follows an organized process (Project Life Cycle PLC)
- Has goals based on specific quality standards
- Utilizes time, money, resources, and the people that are specifically allocated to the project
- Generally has time and cost constraints

A Program

A program is a logical group of related projects managed together in order to achieve decreased risk, economies of scale, and improved management. In a program you will possibly find more than one project manager to complete the work required for each individual project and also a program manager to coordinate and manage these projects.

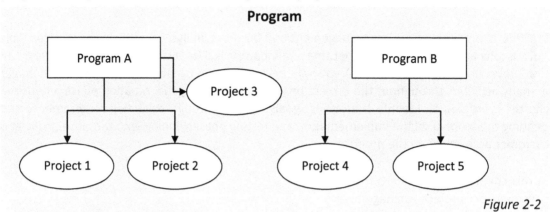

Figure 2-2

A Portfolio

A portfolio is a group of projects or programs that are linked together by a specific strategic business goal. These programs and projects may not be related other than the fact that they are helping to achieve that common strategic goal.

Portfolio management is particularly concerned with the management of resources across competing projects and programs.

Portfolio managers must ensure that senior management is provided with the information they require.

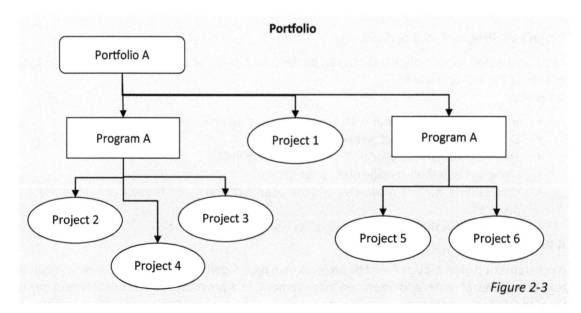

Figure 2-3

Project Management

The Project Management Institute (PMI) defines project management as the application of knowledge, skills, and techniques to project activities to meet the project requirements. It includes directing and coordinating various resources throughout the life of a project in an organized manner.

Project Management Office (PMO)

The department within the organization (not a single person) that centralizes the management of projects, it is responsible for linking corporate strategy to project execution.

The PMO can have various names, depending on the organization and the extent of its role.
- Provide policies, templates and PM methodologies
- Provide support and guidance
- Mentoring and skills development
- Coordinate resource allocation across all projects
- Consolidation and dissemination of lessons learned

The Project Constraints

As a business analyst, you need to be aware of how the project manager handles many things to accomplish a project, including constraints like time, cost, risk, scope, quality, customer satisfaction and resources.

The relationship between the project constraints indicates that if any of these constraints changes, at least one other will be impacted by that change.

- What are the challenges that face the project manager?

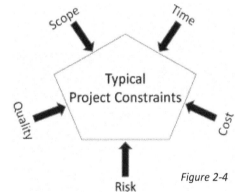

Figure 2-4

Project team members

Because 80% of projects nowadays are IT related, the chances are your team will include the following roles: (remember you could have more than one person in a specific role)
1. *Project sponsor* – the project requestor, the person who initiates the project, he has time, money and resources invested in the project and responsible for the overall project delivery.
2. *Project manager* – the project managers has the responsibility of the planning, execution and closing of the project. Also they are in charge of progress and performance of the project.
3. *Business analyst* – IT business analyst acts as a liaison between technology staff and

business management.

4. *Software development team* – the team could include the following roles:

    i.   Software architect – a person who will develop the design of the software product taking into account customer's requirements. The design architect is a "guru" who is able to work out software architecture for any complex system.

    ii. Designer – a creative person who is responsible for the product look and feel taking into account customer's requirements.

    iii. Software developer – this person will write the actual code.

    iv. Deployment – the deployment role is the one that packages up all of the compiled code and configuration files and deploys it through the appropriate environment or on the appropriate system.

5. Quality Assurance – the inspection, testing and other relevant actions taken to ensure that the desired level of quality is in accordance with the applicable standards or specifications for the product to work.

- In your last project, what were the roles in your team?
- Tell me about your team in your last project.

 Typical team in small to medium projects:

- 1 PM
- 1 – 2 BA's, could be a Lead BA + Sr. BA
- 1 architect – to design the system
- 2-3 developers – to develop the system
- 2 testers (QA) – to perform testing tasks and validate the system
- 1 scheduler or coordinator

Stakeholders:

A stakeholder is *anyone* who has interest in the project (has a stake in the project) or anyone whose interest may be positively or negatively affected by the project or its product, a stakeholder could be:

- Project manager
- Customer or user
- Project team members

- Project management team
- Sponsor
- Internal and external influencers
- Project management office

Identifying stakeholders and creating a Stakeholders Analysis are two critical project activities that you – as a business analyst – will be working on with the project manager during the initiation phase of the project. (this will be explained later in this chapter)

Now think about how you treat the stakeholders in your project. Treating stakeholders means that you keep them informed, solicit their input and work to satisfy their needs and manage their expectations. Without this effort, the project may fail.

BUILD UP YOUR PROJECT MANAGEMENT VOCABULARY

There are several terms project managers always use; it's important as a business analyst to be familiar with them:

1. **WBS (work breakdown structure)** – subdividing work deliverables into smaller more manageable components.

   Features and benefits of WBS:
   - Deliverable oriented hierarchy
   - Created by the PM with the help of the team
   - Deliverables not in the WBS are not part of the project
   - Prevents scope creep
   - Provides a basis for estimating resources, cost, and time
   - Facilitates communication between team members
   - The WBS is the foundation of the project

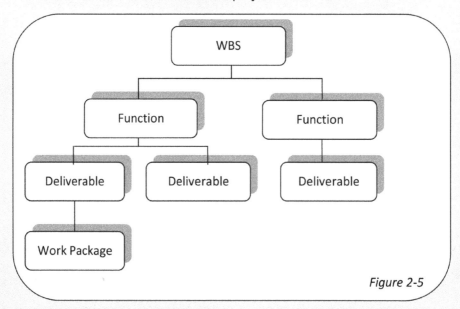

Figure 2-5

2. **Milestones** – significant point or event
3. **Baselines** – approved plans for the project (includes the schedule, budget and requirements artifacts)
4. **Constraints** (sometimes triple constraints) – balancing the time, cost and scope of the project. For example, if you increase the scope it will impact the cost and time of the project
5. **HLE** – High Level Estimates

6. Project Life Cycle (PLC) – there are many different types of project life cycle. According to the Project Management Institute (PMI), the phases of the PLC are:

   1) Initiating
   2) Planning
   3) Executing
   4) Monitoring and controlling
   5) Closing

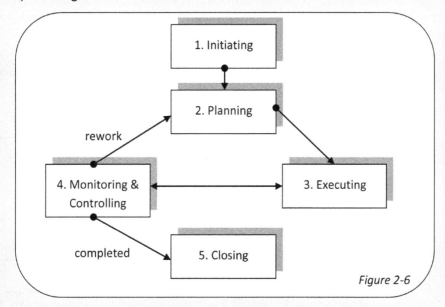

Figure 2-6

7. **Gantt chart** – is a graphical display of the scheduling information, it's effective for progress reporting and control. (MS Project is the most common tool used to create Gantt charts)

8. **CCB (Change Control Board)** – is a group of stakeholders responsible for reviewing and analyzing change requests, the board then approves or rejects changes

9. **Stakeholders** – person or organization *actively involved* whose interest may be positively or negatively impacted by the project or its products

10. **Change management** – it focuses on managing the change in a project. It describes how changes will be managed and controlled so that it does not cause mass chaos.

11. **Risk mitigation** – it's a risk response planning technique associated with threats to reduce probability or impact

12. **Gold plating** – delivering extra features or functionalities that are not documented in the project's scope. Gold plating is considered to be bad because the extra functionality increases risk, cost and time

Organizational Structures

Why do you need to read this section? This section describes every organization that you will be working for. You need to understand the organization structure to know who your boss is, who you report to and who has the power in each type of organization – the project manager or the functional manager.

Functional organization

This is the most common form of organizations. In a functional organization structure, the organization is grouped by areas of specialization within different functional areas. Team members complete project work in addition to normal departmental work.

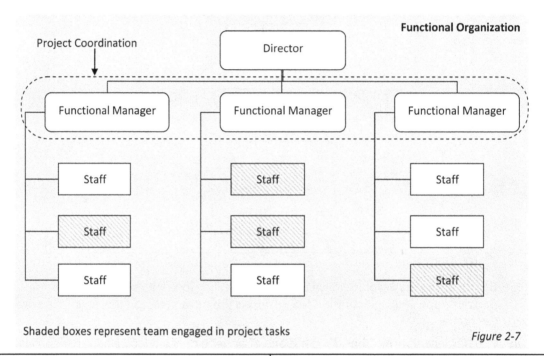

Shaded boxes represent team engaged in project tasks

Figure 2-7

Advantages	Disadvantages
Easier management of specialists	People place more emphasis on their functional specialty to the detriment of the project
Team members report to only one supervisor	Project manager has little or no authority
Similar resources are centralized, the company is grouped by specialties	
Clearly defined career paths	

- In functional organizations, your formal boss is the business analysis manager not the PM. You will still work with and report to the PM, but he is more of a co-worker than a boss.
- Usually the functional manager is the hiring manager.

Projectized organization

In a projectized organization, the entire company is organized by projects, and the project manager has control over the project. Team is assigned and reports to the project manager. Always remember the word "no home" when you think of a projectized organization, where team members do not have a department to go back to when the project is over. They are either assigned to another project or get a job with a different client.

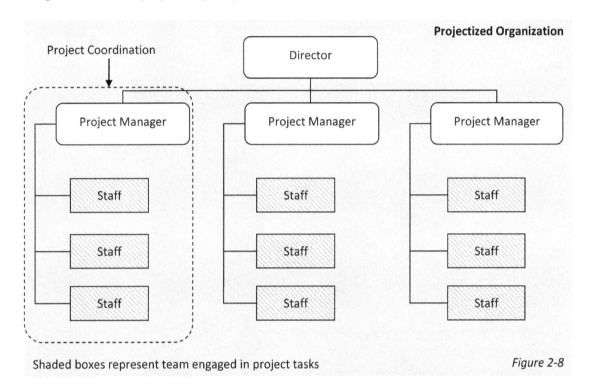

Shaded boxes represent team engaged in project tasks   *Figure 2-8*

- In projectized organizations, your formal boss is the project manager.
- Usually the project manager is the hiring manager.

Matrix organization (Functional + Projectized)

The matrix organization form is an attempt to maximize the strengths of both functional and projectized structures. The keyword to the matrix organization is "two bosses", where team members report to two bosses: the project manager and the functional manager.

The good thing about the matrix structure is that the responsibility is shared between project and functional managers. Both maintain some authority, responsibility and accountability.

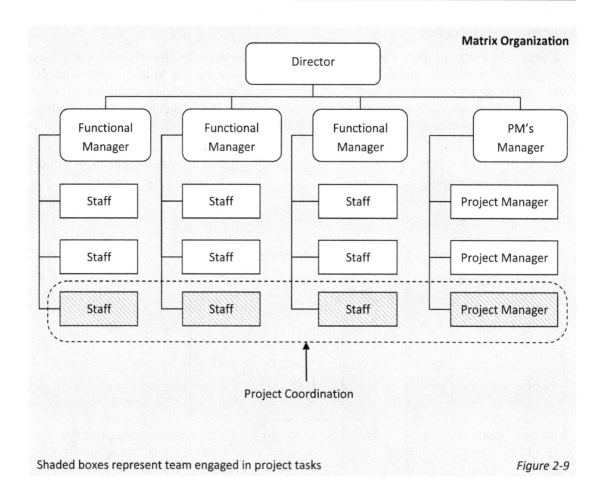

Shaded boxes represent team engaged in project tasks   *Figure 2-9*

- Project manager – controls what the team does and when
- Functional manager (BA manager) – assigns staff and determines the technology to be used

- What was the organization type in your last project? How was it?
- Who did you report to?

HOW TO MANAGE YOUR MANAGER

Remember that no 2 managers are alike, so here are 3 tips to manage your boss:

1. **How? Find out how they think and what they need**

   - Detailed oriented à reports & numbers
   - Results oriented àaction & deliverables

2. **What you need and how they can support you**

   - Intuitive person à trust & gut feel (Hey, I need you to trust me)
   - Innovative person à new ways to do things (I have a new idea or new template that you might like)

3. **Set expectations**

   - It's ok to say "don't bug me every 5 minutes, trust me I'll get it done" and agree on another way to get them informed.
   - Let them know if you need "prep time"
   - Let them know how its best to communicate with you (email or phone, etc)
   - Communicate your priorities
   - Ask for support if needed (you would need to escalate some issues you might face)

Project Management Knowledge Areas

Knowledge areas as defined by PMI (according to the PMBOK 4th edition)

1. Integration management – keeping everyone working toward the same goal and dealing with change
2. Scope management – defining the work that needs to be done on the project (eliciting requirements and developing a detailed description of the project and product)
3. Time management – creating the project timeline, deadlines and milestones
4. Cost management – developing cost baseline and estimating the budget
5. Quality management – identifying the quality standards of the project based on the customer's requirements
6. Human resources management – identifying the project roles, responsibilities and required skills and creating a staffing management plan
7. Communications management – determining who should talk to whom, when and how often
8. Risk management – defining possible risks and developing a mitigation plan
9. Procurement management – defining contracts and choosing contractors to do work for the project

Quick TIP
   - Risk is any unplanned incident that has positive or negative impact.

As a business analyst you will be involved with the project manager in the following knowledge areas:
- Scope management
- Time management
- Risk management
- Communications management (stakeholders management)

The life of a project

After the project charter is created by the sponsors, the project manager starts developing the team and hiring people, usually the business analyst is the first person to join the team after the project manager. The BA then works with the project manager on identifying the project stakeholders and creating the stakeholders register which is basically a list of all the project stakeholders prioritized according to their importance, impact, and interest to the project.

Now that the charter and stakeholders register are created, the business analyst can start his/her main role of collecting, analyzing and documenting requirements and create the requirements management plan (RMP), business requirements document (BRD), and functional requirements document (FRD). Then work with the project manager on defining the detailed project scope and decompose the scope into smaller more manageable components to create the work breakdown structure. (*figure 2-5*)

The project manager – with some involvement of the business analyst – starts working on decomposing the work packages in the WBS one more level into activities to be able to sequence them and estimate the resources and duration needed to complete them and develop the project schedule. Also as we are still in the planning phase of the project, the project manager will work on developing the risk management plan, quality management plan, human resources plan, cost baseline (budget) and the procurement plan. All that is compiled into the project management plan (PMP).

In the execution phase, the business analyst usually supports the development team and provides answers and clarifications about the requirements. There is not much involvement with the project management activities.

In the monitoring and controlling phase, the business analyst works on the change management process to control the impact of any change request from the business or development team. After the coding is completed the business analyst works with the testers in verifying the scope and making sure that all the requirements are completed successfully before delivering the project to the customer.

The last phase of the project is to deliver the project to the customer and perform the user acceptance testing at the client's location to close the project and make sure the customer is satisfied. In some organizations you may be asked to help train the business users and create help documentation and user manuals.

In table 2-1, you can see all the 42 project management activities as defined in the Project Management Body Of Knowledge 4th edition (PMBOK) by PMI. The highlighted cells indicate the areas of overlap in both roles of business analysis and project management.

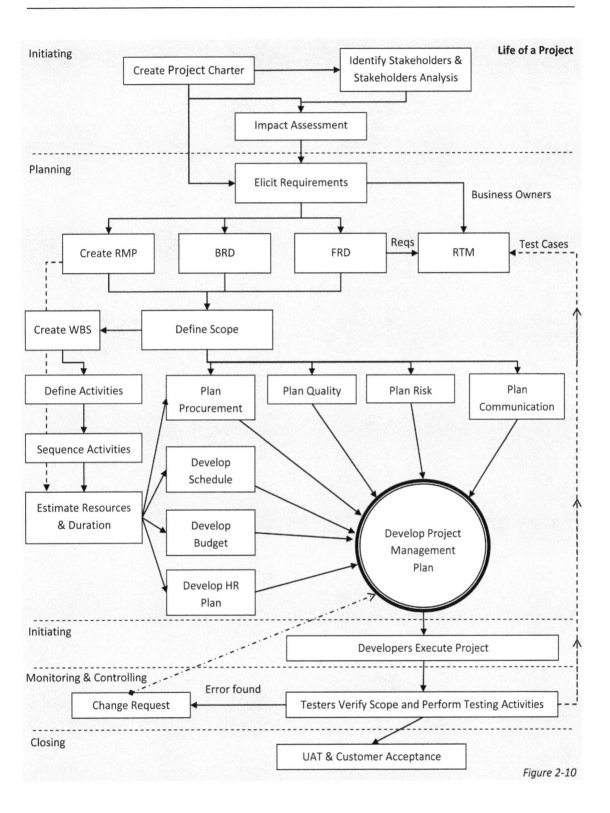

Figure 2-10

Phase / Knowledge area	I. Initiating	II. Planning	III. Executing	IV. Monitoring & Controlling	V. Closing
1. Integration Management	• Develop project charter	• Develop project management plan	• Manage project execution	• Perform change management	• Close project • (Deliver project to customer & perform UAT)
2. Scope Management		• Collect requirements • Define scope • Create WBS		• Verify scope • (testing) • Control scope	
3. Time Management		• Define activities • Sequence activities • Estimate resources • Estimate duration • Develop schedule		• Control schedule	
4. Quality Management		• Plan quality	• Quality assurance	• Quality control	
5. Communication Management	• Identify stakeholders • Stakeholders analysis	• Plan communication	• Distribute information • Manage stakeholders expectations	• Report performance	
6. Cost Management		• Estimate cost • Determine budget		• Control cost	
7. Human Resources Management		• Develop HR plan	• Acquire team • Develop team • Manage team		
8. Risk Management		• Plan risk mgmt. • Identify risks • Qualitative risk analysis • Quantitative risk analysis • Plan risk responses		• Monitor and control risks	
9. Procurement Management		• Plan procurements	• Conduct procurements	• Administer procurements	• Close procurements

Table 2-1

Intersecting activities between the BA and PM

Develop project charter

As a BA, you may join the project after the project charter is created, but it is still very important to understand what a project charter is, why it is important, and how it is used throughout the life of a project. You will use the charter as high level requirements when you elicit the detailed requirements from the business and define the scope.

The charter *formally recognizes* the project (gives the green light for the project to begin). **Without the charter, the project does not exist.**

Typical contents include:

Project Title or Name

Project Description

What is the project?

Project Manager Assigned and Authority level

(PM Name) shall be the project manager for this project and have the authority to develop the project schedule and budget.

Business Case
What is the purpose of the project? Why it is worth the investment? and what is the problem it will be solving? What is the Return on investment ROI?

Resources Assigned
Who is assigned to the project and what are their roles?

Stakeholders
Any person or organization that the project will have a positive or negative impact on them

Stakeholders Requirements

This can be considered the high level requirements that you will be using when you are defining the project scope.

Project Success Criteria

Summary Milestone schedule
Due no later than October 18, 20XX

Summary budget

Project Approval Requirements
Who will sign-off the business requirements and functional specifications?

Who will sign-off the project schedule?

Identifying stakeholders

The attitude and actions of stakeholders can have a significant effect on the performance and outcome of the project and must be managed. This is primarily the responsibility of the project manager, although the BA shares responsibility with the PM because you will spend most of your time with the business stakeholders to elicit their requirements.

These are the potential stakeholders that you need to indentify in your project:
- Regulatory bodies
- Your project team
- Business SME's
- Client/sponsor
- End user
- Business requirements owners
- Approvers

- You need to know who is approving your documents to make sure to capture their requirements, sometimes you elicit the owners' requirements and the approvers do not approve your BRD because they were not involved in the elicitation sessions.

Let's say you just got assigned to a project and today is your first day. How do you identify the project stakeholders to start collecting their requirements?

These are the steps I would follow:

1. Use the initial list of stakeholders from the project charter
2. Use any contracts related to the project as a starting point
3. Records from the past projects lessons learned (in many organizations they have the same SME's)
4. Reach out to the PM and ask directly, "Who should I invite to this meeting?"
5. Now that you have a list of stakeholders, it may be too high level list or outdated. Reach out to them to confirm – they may suggest other stakeholders to include

Manage stakeholder expectations

As simple as this process might sound, managing stakeholder's expectations is the one major factor that will make you stand out from the rest of the crowd. The stakeholders could be your boss, the project manager, your team members, senior management in your organization, and the business SME from whom you are eliciting the requirements.

Managing stakeholder expectations requires:
- Building trust (You do not always have to say things are perfect)
- Resolving conflicts
- Active listening
- Walking them through what will occur to make sure they do not have unrealistic expectations

- Management skills, such as presentation skills, negotiation skills, and public speaking
- Avoiding communication blockers, such as language, culture, making negative statements, noisy surroundings (Conflicts occur due to lack of communication)

Kickoff meeting

Once all the stakeholders are identified, the stakeholder register is created to define all the parties involved in the project and prioritized according to their impact and interest to the project, a **kickoff meeting** should be held before starting to work on collecting customer's requirements and defining the scope.

The kickoff meeting involves all the project stakeholders (e.g., customer, the project team, senior management, functional management, the sponsor) to announce the start of the project and ensure that everyone is familiar with its details. Make sure everyone is on the same page and introduce who is involved in the project.
The kickoff meeting includes a high level plan of the following:

- Project goals and objectives
- Milestones
- Risks
- Schedule
- Cost
- Communication management plan

Project Scope Management

Collect requirements
This activity describes the main role of a BA. Here is where you will be creating the requirements management plan (RMP), business requirements document (BRD) and the requirements traceability matrix (RTM). Collecting requirements will be discussed thoroughly in the requirements chapter, but here are the requirements gathering tools as described in the PMBOK.

- Interviews
- Focus groups
- Facilitated workshops
- Group creativity techniques
- Group decision making techniques
- Questionnaires and surveys
- Observation (job shadowing)
- Prototypes

Define scope

It is the process of defining what is and is not included in the project and its deliverables. In this process the project manager will use the requirements documentation you created in the Collect Requirements process, the project charter and any additional information needed to define the project scope.

Remember that defining the scope is an iterative process, especially if time, money or other constraints limit the ability to deliver all the scope. The project manager my need to negotiate with stakeholders to re-define the scope during the project if the resulting schedule or budget do not meet the sponsor's or management's expectations – which means that you might need to re-collect the requirements.

The project scope should include:
- Project objectives
- Project boundaries – what is in scope and what is out of scope
- Deliverables and specifications
- Acceptance criteria
- Constraints
- Assumptions
- Dependencies

After the scope is defined and baselined, any change to scope must be evaluated for its impact on schedule, budget, risks and quality. (Will be discussed in the change management section)

- While you are collecting the requirements, you ALWAYS need to determine what is and is not included in the project scope and remember that **Gold Plating** a project (adding extras) is not allowed.

Verify scope

Verifying the scope happens in the monitoring and controlling phase (see figure 2-10), it is the performance of acceptance testing with the customer to verify that the finished product is in compliance with their requirements.

- It is helpful to have the approved scope with you when you meet with the customer.
- Another thing you will need to have is the requirements traceability matrix, so you can track where requirements came from and prove that require-ments were completed.

Now do not get confused between the QA testing process that happens internally to each work package and verifying the scope with the customer or end user to gain formal acceptance of deliverables. In figure 2-11 you will see how Verify Scope relates to Testing activity.

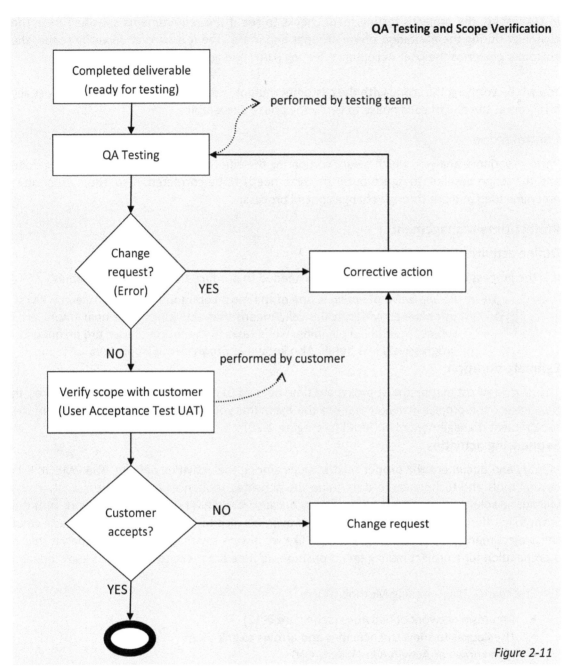

QA Testing and Scope Verification

Completed deliverable (ready for testing)

performed by testing team

QA Testing

Change request? (Error)

YES

Corrective action

NO

performed by customer

Verify scope with customer (User Acceptance Test UAT)

Customer accepts?

NO

Change request

YES

Figure 2-11

Generally QA testing is done first to make sure the deliverable meets the requirements before it is presented to the customer. Both processes are very similar in that both involve testing the conformance of deliverables with requirements. The difference is the focus of the effort and who is doing the testing.

In QA testing, the project's testing team checks to see if the requirements specified from the customer during the elicitation phase are met and make sure it is correct. In verify scope, the customer performs the User Acceptance Testing (UAT) and accepts the deliverables.

You will be verifying the scope with the customer multiple times in your project, because usually it is done at the end of each phase to verify the phase deliverables.

Control scope

Perform variance analysis, which means comparing the difference between the work being done and the scope baseline to figure out if the plan needs to be corrected. If so, the correction is recommended and put through change control process.

Project Time Management

Define activities

It is the process of determining the activities needed to produce the project deliverables.

- *Rolling wave planning* is one of the most common techniques used by PM's to define activities. It basically means that activities in the near future are subject to detailed planning, while tasks in the future phases are planned in progressively less detail. Also known as *Progressive Elaboration*.

Estimate duration

The process of estimating the approximate time needed to complete the identified activities. In this process the project manager will use the estimates you provided for your activities in the requirement management plan (RMP) (see figure 2-10).

Sequencing activities

Identify and document the proper relationships among the activities defined. The PMBOK lists several tools and techniques to determine the activities sequence. As a business analyst you will not be solely accountable for this activity because it is a PM responsibility to work with the team to get their inputs for each activity. However, it's nice to know on a high level basis what the project manager will be doing, because like we always say that the business analyst role is a preparation for a project management position, so here are these tools for your knowledge:

1. Precedence Diagramming Method (PDM)

    - Creates a network of activities (see figure 2-12)
    - Uses boxes to show the activities and arrows to link them
    - Also known as Activity-On-Node (AON)
    - There are four major activity relationships: (see figure 2-13)

Determine dependencies

- Mandatory dependency (Hard logic)
- Discretionary dependency (Soft logic or preferred)
- External dependency (external party like government or suppliers)

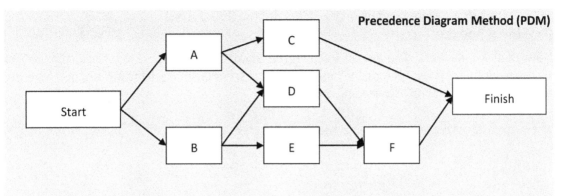

Figure 2-12

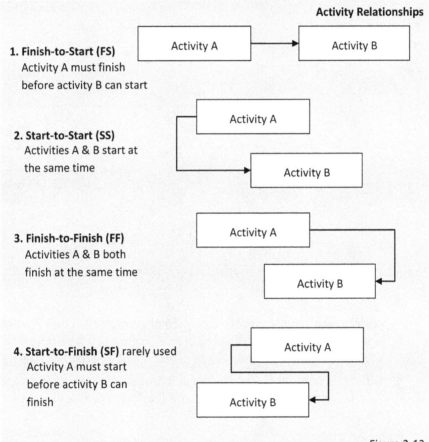

Figure 2-13

2. Apply leads and lags

- A **Lead** starts an activity before its predecessor is finished – for example, starting to create a prototype 5 days before the design is complete (FS – 5 days)
- A **Lag** is a delay before a successor activity can begin – for example, letting concrete set

for 3 days before building on it – it is wait time (FS + 3 days)

Develop schedule

Now that the network diagram and activity duration estimates are completed, the project manager will put this information into a schedule. The schedule pulls all the information together to predict the proje ct milestones and end date.

Microsoft Project is the most common tool used to develop a schedule:

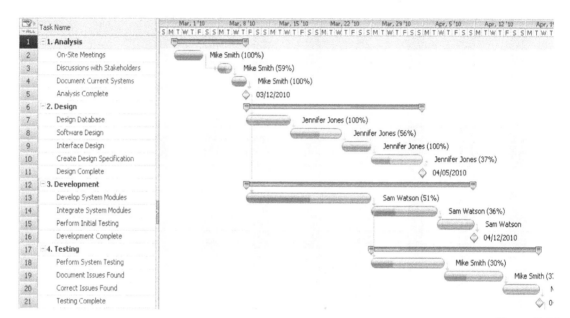

Figure 2-14

- **Critical path** – is the longest sequence of activities through the network diagram. Activities on the critical path must happen on time where the delay of any activity on the critical path affects the whole schedule. (see figure 2-15)

- The project cannot be completed in a time shorter than the critical path duration. In example 2-15, 27 days is the shortest time it could take to complete the project.

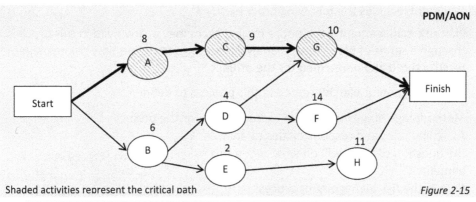

Shaded activities represent the critical path   *Figure 2-15*

Network Paths	Path Duration
A-C-G	8+9+10 = 27
B-D-G	6+4+10 = 20
B-D-F	6+4+14 = 24
B-E-H	6+2+11 = 19

Schedule compression

There are two primary schedule compression techniques that you will come across constantly in your projects as a BA:

- Crashing – basically means adding more resources to shorten the duration of activities on the critical path. Crashing always adds COST. For example, adding more developers to complete a certain activity in 2 weeks instead of 3 weeks.
- Fast tracking – re-planning activities (or phases) initially planned to occur in sequence, but instead will be done in the same time (in parallel) to save time.

Project Communication Management

Plan Communication activity is explained in chapter 3 (Requirements Communication)

Project Risk Management

This section describes an overview of project risk management and some basic risk management terms and concepts. As a BA you need to understand these to prepare yourself to deal with the project risks that you may face in real world situations.

Remember, high level risks are identified in the project charter in the initiation phase and are continuously kept up to date throughout the project phases. The project manager works with the team on identifying the risks and look at what has happened on the project, the current status, and what is yet to come and reassess the potential threats and opportunities.

- What is risk? *Risk is any uncertain event or condition that, if it occurs, has an effect on at least one project objective (scope, schedule, cost, quality, etc.). A risk may or may not actually happen; if it does, it becomes an issue.*

Risk management includes the following processes:

1. Plan risk management – the entire project team may be involved in this process through a series of planning and analysis meetings to define how risk management will be structured and performed for the project.

   Risk management plan is created in this process to define:

- Methodology of performing risk management for the project
- Assigning roles and responsibilities to answer the question of "who will do what when this risk happens?"
- Cost of the risk management process
- When and how often risk management cycle will be performed
- Categorizing risks to help ensure areas of risk are not forgotten in the project
- How risks will be reported and tracked

> *Up to 90% of the threats identified and investigated in the risk management process can be eliminated.*

Define the probability of the occurrence of the risk and its impact on the project to be able to calculate the Expected Monetary Value (EMV) of a risk

> EMV = Probability (P) X Impact (I)
>
> EMV = 10% X $20,000 = $2,000

Analyze risk by answering the following questions:

- What is the risk?
- What would cause the risk?
- What are the consequences of it happening? What is the impact?
- How likely? (The probability that it will occur)
- When is it expected to occur?
- How often? (The expected frequency of occurrence)

Example, there is a <u>risk</u> that the customer will be unable to complete acceptance testing in a timely fashion, <u>caused</u> by their lack of experience in this area, <u>resulting</u> in delayed payment. This is expected to happen <u>three</u> times in the <u>verify scope process</u>.

2. Identify risks – the process of determining which risk events might affect the project

(what can go wrong?). This process should be carried out at the start of the project and then reviewed regularly throughout the project life cycle.

3.   Perform qualitative risk analysis – potential impact of risks needs to be prioritized because not all risks identified are worth doing something about. It could have minor impact on the project and be too expensive to fix. In this process, risks are categorized according to their impact, urgency, and probability.

		Impact				
		Trivial	**Minor**	**Moderate**	**Major**	**Extreme**
Probability	**Rare**	Low	Low	Low	Medium	Medium
	Unlikely	Low	Low	Medium	Medium	Medium
	Moderate	Low	Medium	Medium	Medium	High
	Likely	Medium	Medium	Medium	High	High
	Very Likely	Medium	Medium	High	High	High

4.   Perform quantitative risk analysis – to analyze numerically the probability and impact of each risk and determine which risk worth taking action.

5.   Plan risk responses – now that all the possible risks are identified and prioritized according to their impact and probability, we need to determine what are we going to do about each top risk.

- Are all risks bad? This is a tricky question. To answer this question we need to go back to the risk definition in PMBOK. Risk is any uncertain event that could have a positive or negative impact. Uncertain event could be a threat or opportunity; the goal is to eliminate some threats and reduce the probability and impact of others and enhance opportunities.

- Opportunity could be: if we buy the materials for a certain work package before the prices increase in October 2014, the cost will be 20% less than planned.

Strategies for negative risk or threat

- **Avoid** – involves changing the project management plan to eliminate the threat entirely by eliminating the cause (e.g., replace a developer who is expected to leave the team during the project execution or even removing a work package entirely). Some risks that arise early in the project can be avoided by clarifying requirements or obtaining detailed information.

> **Transfer or deflect the risk** – ways in which you can attempt to pass the responsibility of the risk to another party:
>
>   o   Use a warranty
>
>   o   Purchase insurance
>
>   o   Outsourcing of high risk work packages
>
>   o   Using subcontractor with back to back agreement (e.g. passing penalties imposed by the client on to the subcontractors)

- **Mitigate, control or reduce the risk** – including actions within the project plan to reduce the probability of the risk happening and/or its impact. Another form of mitigation is putting contingency plans in place, such that if the risk event occurs, it reduces its impact. (e.g. adding 2 weeks contingency to the testing work package in the project schedule to mitigate the risk of losing a sick tester).
- **Accept** – can be used for both threats and opportunities. Accepting the risk strategy is used because it is impossible to eliminate all the identified risks in the project. As we mentioned earlier in the qualitative risk analysis process, not all risks are worth doing something about due to their very low impact on the project. This strategy indicates that the risk is acknowledged but no action will take place – If it happens, it happens.

Strategies for positive risk or opportunity

- **Exploit (opposite of avoid)** – making sure the opportunity occurs and making the most out of this opportunity
- **Enhance** – by increasing the likelihood
- **Share** – bringing in a third party with more expertise, or forming a partnership that is best to achieve the opportunity

- **Workarounds** – unplanned responses created to deal with unexpected treats or for which no mitigation plan is developed.

Identifying risks (SWOT ANALYSIS)

The main objective of the technique is to study the strength, weakness, opportunities and threats and improve the state of the organization by:

- Using or capitalizing the strengths
- Recognizing and improve weaknesses
- Exploit the Opportunities
- Work around the threats either to avoid them or turn them into advantages.

Strengths and Weakness can be analyzed in terms of organizations Resources, Core Competencies, Performance and Portfolio

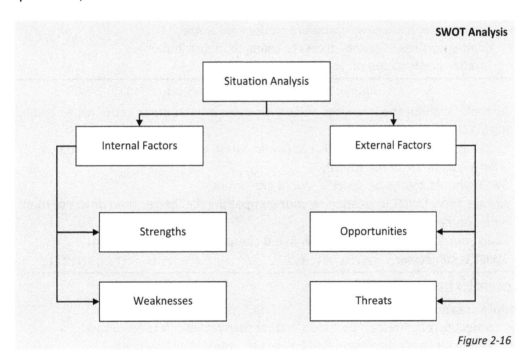

Figure 2-16

Strengths and weaknesses are internal factors.

Strength could be:

- Your specialist marketing expertise
- A new, innovative product or service
- Location of your business
- Quality processes and procedures
- Any other aspect of your business that adds value to your product or service

A weakness could be:

- Lack of marketing expertise
- Undifferentiated products or services (i.e. in relation to your competitors)
- Location of your business
- Poor quality goods or services

- Damaged reputation

Opportunities and threats are external factors.

An opportunity could be:

- A developing market such as the Internet
- Mergers, joint ventures or strategic alliances
- Moving into new market segments that offer improved profits
- A new international market
- A market vacated by an ineffective competitor

A threat could be:

- A new competitor in your home market
- Price wars with competitors
- A competitor has a new, innovative product or service
- Competitors have superior access to channels of distribution
- Taxation is introduced on your product or service

Rules for successful SWOT analysis

- Be realistic about the strengths and weaknesses of your organization when conducting SWOT analysis.
- SWOT analysis should distinguish between where your organization is today, and where it could be in the future.
- SWOT should always be specific. Avoid grey areas.
- Always apply SWOT in relation to your competition i.e. better than or worse than your competition.
- Keep your SWOT short and simple. Avoid complexity and over analysis.
- SWOT is subjective.

Risk examples from real time IT projects

Schedule creation risks

- Schedule is optimistic, "best case," rather than realistic, "expected case"
- Product is larger than estimated (in lines of code or function points)
- A delay in one task causes cascading delays in dependent tasks
- Target date is moved up with no corresponding adjustment to the product scope or available resources

Organization and management risks

- Budget cuts upset project plans
- Layoffs and cutbacks reduce team's capacity
- Management review/decision cycle is slower than expected

End User

- End user insists on new requirements
- End user ultimately finds product to be unsatisfactory, requiring redesign and rework
- End user input is not solicited, so product ultimately fails to meet user expectations and must be reworked

Requirements

- Requirements have been base lined but continue to change
- Requirements are poorly defined, and further definition expands the scope of the project
- Additional requirements are added
- Vaguely specified areas of the product are more time-consuming than expected

Design and implementation

- Inappropriate design leads to redesign and re-implementation
- Components developed separately cannot be integrated easily, requiring redesign and rework
- Process
- Amount of paperwork results in slower progress than expected
- Inaccurate progress tracking results in not knowing the project is behind schedule until late in the project

External environment

- Product depends on government regulations, which change unexpectedly

Customer

- Customer insists on new requirements
- Customer micro-manages the development process, resulting in slower progress than planned
- Customer-mandated support tools and environments are incompatible, have poor performance, or have inadequate functionality, resulting in reduced productivity
- Customer will not accept the software as delivered even though it meets all specifications

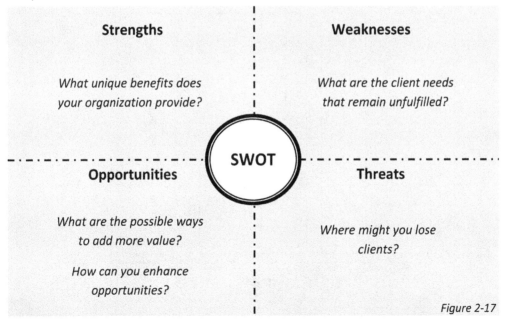

Figure 2-17

Perform change management

It is the process of handling change requests to any part of the project. Remember that just because the change is requested, this does not mean that it has to be implemented. This is where change management process comes in place. The requested change must be evaluated to understand its impact on the overall project by the Change Control Board (CCB) and accepted or rejected before it is implemented.

The business analyst plays a major role in the change management process. To fully understand this process we need to be aware of the following definitions:

- Change request – it is a formal request submitted by a downstream work package to change work done by an upstream work package. A change could be modification in requirements (add, remove or update), design, scope or even policies and procedures
- Change control board (CCB) – a designated group who evaluates the change request's impact on the project and the organization and approves or rejects the request
- Corrective action – when a change request is accepted by the CCB, it is time to take corrective actions to implement that change
- Preventive action – some preventive actions like changing a resource or schedule take place to deal with anticipated deviations from the project management plan or possible risks
- Change log – records all change requests and keeps track of status
- Cost of change – the cost of a change is least expensive in the early stages of the project

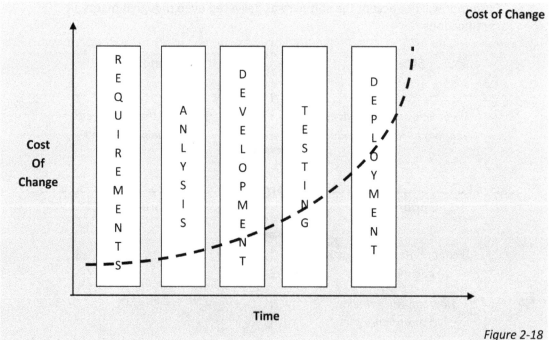

Figure 2-18

- Walk me through the change management process.
- One of the business SME's wants to make a change to the requirements or the scope, what are you going to do?

What should I do when I get a change request?

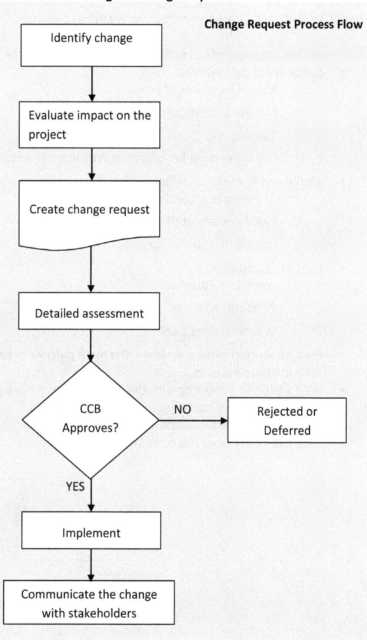

Change Request Process Flow

Identify change

Evaluate impact on the project

Create change request

Detailed assessment

CCB Approves? — NO → Rejected or Deferred

YES

Implement

Communicate the change with stakeholders

Figure 2-19

Close project or phase

It is the process of finalizing the project, obtaining formal acceptance and handing over the final product, service or result that the project was authorized to produce. The acceptance includes receipt of a formal statement that the terms of the contract have been met, issue the final lessons learned, and index and archive all the project records.

Let's have a look at some of the activities in the close project process:
- Handover of deliverables
  - Formal handover of product
  - Maintenance procedures
  - Training
  - Handover must be formal and recorded to ensure transfer of responsibilities
- Admin and financial closeout
  - Archiving of project files
  - Client documentation
  - Complete financial closure
- Contract completion
  - Formal acceptance
  - Payments received
  - Subcontractors paid
- Prepare for post-project review – the main purpose is to record lessons learned to be used in future projects
- Hold a close-out meeting with the client or senior management to formally close the project and ensure there are no outstanding issues
- Complete final performance reporting
- Solicit feedback from the customer about the project

see table 2-1

I. Initiating Phase

❖ 1. INTEGRATION MANAGEMENT

- **Project Charter:** formally recognizes the project
  - ○ Project Description
  - ○ Project Manager Assigned and Authority level
  - ○ Business Case
  - ○ Resources Assigned
  - ○ Stakeholders
  - ○ Stakeholders Requirements
  - ○ Project Success Criteria
  - ○ Summary Milestone schedule
  - ○ Summary budget
  - ○ Project Approval Requirements

❖ 5. COMMUNICATION MANAGEMENT

- **A Stakeholder could be:**
  - ○ Client/Sponsor   ○ Req. Owner   ○ Team Members
  - ○ End User   ○ Approvers   ○ SME's
- **Managing stakeholder expectations requires:**
  - ○ Building trust
  - ○ Resolving conflicts
  - ○ Active listening
  - ○ Walking them through what will occur to make sure they do not have unrealistic expectations
  - ○ Management skills, such as presentation skills, negotiation skills, and public speaking
  - ○ Avoiding communication blockers
- **Kickoff meeting** is held to announce the start of the project and ensure that everyone is familiar with its details. It includes a high level plan of the following:
  - ○ Goals & Objectives   ○ Milestones   ○ Risks
  - ○ Schedule   ○ Cost   ○ Communication

II. Planning Phase

❖ 2. SCOPE MANAGEMENT

- **Collect requirements** is the process where the BA elicits the business SME's requirements and create the requirements artifacts (RMP, BRD, RTM, etc.)
- **Define Scope** is the process of defining what is and is not included in the project and its deliverables. The scope document should include the following:
  - ○ objectives   ○ constraints   ○ Project boundaries
  - ○ Assumptions   ○ Dependencies   ○ Acceptance criteria

- **Organization Structures**
  - ○ In a *functional organization* structure, the organization is grouped by areas of specialization within different functional areas. Team members complete project work in addition to normal departmental work.
  - ○ In a *projectized organization*, the entire company is organized by projects, and the project manager has control over the project. Team is assigned and reports to the project manager.
  - ○ The *matrix organization* form is an attempt to maximize the strengths of both functional and projectized structures. The keyword to the matrix organization is *"two bosses"*, where team members report to two bosses: the project manager and the functional manager.
- **Project management knowledge areas (PMBOK 4th):**
  1. Integration management: keeping everyone working toward the same goal & dealing with change
  2. Scope management: defining the work that needs to be done (eliciting requirements & developing a detailed description of the project & product)
  3. Time management: creating the project timeline, deadlines & milestones
  4. Quality management: identifying the quality standards based on the customer's requirements
  5. Communications management: determining who should talk to whom, how, when & how often
  6. Cost management: developing cost baseline & estimating the budget
  7. Human resources management: identifying the project roles, responsibilities & required skills & creating a staffing management plan
  8. Risk management: defining possible risks & developing a mitigation plan
  9. Procurement management: defining contracts & choosing contractors to do work for the project
- **Project Life Cycle Phases (PMBOK 4th):**

I. Initiate → II. Plan → III. Execute → IV. Monitor & Control → V. Close

---

- **Project** is a temporary endeavour with a beginning and an end to create a unique product, service, or result.
- **Program** is a logical group of related projects managed together in order to achieve decreased risk, economies of scale, and improved management
- **Portfolio** is a group of projects or programs that are linked together by a specific strategic business goal. These programs and projects may not be related other than the fact that they are helping to achieve that common strategic goal
- **Project management** is the application of knowledge, skills, and techniques to project activities to meet the project requirements. It includes directing and coordinating various resources throughout the life of a project in an organized manner
- **Project Management Office (PMO)** is department within the organization (not a single person) that centralizes the management of projects; it is responsible for linking corporate strategy to project execution
- **Stakeholder** is anyone who has interest in the project (has a stake in the project) or anyone whose interest may be positively or negatively affected by the project or its product.
- **Typical team contains of:**
  - ○ 1 PM   ○ 1 Architect   ○ 2 Testers
  - ○ 1-2 BA's   ○ 2-3 Developers   ○ 1 Coordinator
- **WBS (work breakdown structure)** is subdividing work deliverables into smaller more manageable components.
- **Change Management:** it focuses on managing the change in a project. It describes how changes will be managed and controlled so that it does not cause mass chaos
- **Gold plating** is delivering extra features or functionalities that are not documented in the project's scope. Gold plating is considered to be bad because the extra functionality increases risk, cost and time
- **CCB (Change Control Board)** is a group of stakeholders responsible for reviewing and analyzing change requests, the board then approves or rejects changes
- **A Stakeholder** is any person or organization *actively involved* whose interest may be positively or negatively impacted by the project or its products
- **Risk mitigation** is a risk response planning technique associated with threats to reduce probability or impact

❖ 3. TIME MANAGEMENT

- **Define activities** is the process of determining the activities needed to produce the project deliverables (Rolling wave planning is one of the most common techniques used by PM's to define activities. Aka Progressive Elaboration)
- **Estimating duration** is the process of estimating the approximate time needed to complete the identified activities
- **Sequencing activities** is to identify and document the proper relationships among the activities defined using several tools, such as:
  - Precedence Diagramming Method (PDM)
  - Determine dependence
  - Apply Leads and Lags
- **Develop schedule** is the process where the PM compiles the information gathered from the previous activity into a project schedule *(Ms Project is the most common tool used to develop a schedule)*

Schedule Definitions

  - **Critical path** is the longest sequence of activities through the network diagram
  - **Crashing** is a schedule compression tool by adding more resources to shorten the duration of activities on the critical path
  - **Fast tracking** is another schedule compression tool by re-planning activities initially planned to occur in sequence, but instead will be done in the same time (in parallel) to save time

❖ 5. COMMUNICATION MANAGEMENT

- **Plan communication** is the process of planning the communication needs throughout the project

❖ 8. RISK MANAGEMENT

- **Risk** is any uncertain event or condition that, if it occurs, has an effect on at least one project objective (scope, schedule, cost, quality, etc.)
- A risk may or may not actually happen; if it does, it becomes an issue
- **Risk management plan** is created to define how risk will be managed throughout the project and who will do what when risk occurs
- **Identify risks** is the process of determining which risk events might affect the project (what can go wrong?)

- **Perform qualitative risk analysis** to categorize risks according to their impact, urgency, and probability
- **Perform quantitative risk analysis** to analyze numerically the probability and impact of each risk and determine which risk worth taking action
- **Plan risk responses** to determine what are we going to do about each top risk
- **Strategies for negative risk or threat:**
  - Avoid   ○ Transfer
  - Mitigate   ○ Accept
- **Strategies for positive risk or opportunities:**
  - Exploit   ○ Enhance
  - Share   ○ Accept

III. Executing Phase

In the execution phase, the business analyst usually supports the development team and provides answers and clarifications about the requirements. There is not much involvement with the project management activities.

IV. Monitoring & Controlling Phase

❖ 1. INTEGRATION MANAGEMENT

- **Change management** is the process of handling change requests to any part of the project
  - **Change request** is a formal request submitted by a downstream work package to change work done by an upstream work package
  - A **corrective action** is taken to fix the defect or error or to implement a change
  - A **preventive action** is taken to deal with anticipated deviations from the project plan or possible risks
  - A **Change log** records all change requests and keeps track of status

❖ 2. SCOPE MANAGEMENT

- **Verify scope activity** is the performance of acceptance testing with the customer to verify that the finished product is in compliance with their requirements
- **Control scope** is comparing the difference between the work being done and the scope baseline to figure out if the plan needs to be corrected. If so, the correction is recommended and put through change control process

---

V. Closing Phase

- **Closing project or activity** is the process of finalizing the project, obtaining formal acceptance and handing over the final product, service or result that the project was authorized to produce.

PROJECT MANAGER VS BUSINESS ANALYST

PM	BA
• "Project management is the application of knowledge, skills, tools, and techniques to a broad range of activities in order to meet the requirements of a particular project." *(PMBOK® Guide)*	• "Business Analysis is the discipline of identifying the business needs and determining solutions to business problems" *(BABOK® Guide)*
• The PM is usually the first person assigned to the project	• The BA is usually assigned to the project after is has started
• Defines the project scope	• Defines solution scope
• Accountable for delivering a product on time and within budget	• Ensures the product is built right according to the requirements
• Develops the Project Plan and ensures the team follows the plan	• Develops the Requirement Management Plan
• Manages people, money and risk	• Manages requirements
• See the big picture	• Detail-oriented
• Support his/her team to get things done	• Helps SMEs describe how and why they perform tasks
• Manages change requests	• Manages requirements change requests
• String management skills	• Strong investigative skills

The healthy conflict of interest between a PM and BA:
The PM is always pushing to move forward and the BA cautiously wanting to gather just one more detail before going forward—that makes the combination so successful.

3

Requirements Management & Communication

I. Requirements Management

B efore you start reading this chapter, take a moment to ask yourself what requirements management means. You might be surprised to learn that most business analysts get confused when answering this question, or let's say they all have different descriptions of requirements management.

To conclude a comprehensive definition of requirements management in three simple steps: Requirements management is the process of eliciting requirements from the business then analyzing the gathered requirements and presenting them in a way that clearly communicates to the stakeholders.

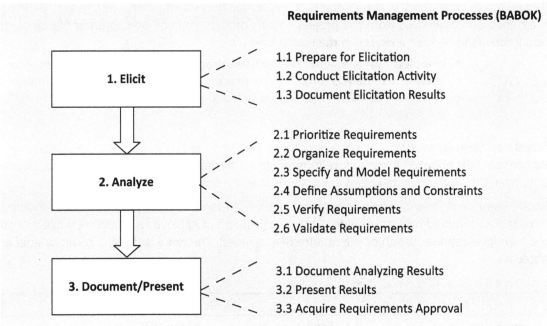

Requirements Management Processes (BABOK)

1. Elicit
1.1 Prepare for Elicitation
1.2 Conduct Elicitation Activity
1.3 Document Elicitation Results

2. Analyze
2.1 Prioritize Requirements
2.2 Organize Requirements
2.3 Specify and Model Requirements
2.4 Define Assumptions and Constraints
2.5 Verify Requirements
2.6 Validate Requirements

3. Document/Present
3.1 Document Analyzing Results
3.2 Present Results
3.3 Acquire Requirements Approval

Figure 3-1

This chapter talks about the core of the business analysis role, which is *eliciting*, *analyzing* and *documenting* requirements from the business. Note that we did not say just document requirements, because this is one of the common mistakes of most BA's and we will be talking about it later in this chapter. You should always remember that the BA must:

1. **Elicit** requirements from the business, by conducting requirements elicitation meetings, JAD sessions, interviewing, etc.

2. **Analyze** the gathered requirements: this means prioritize, organize, specify, verify and validate requirements by identifying the following:

> *"Business Analysts consider a problem, find the root cause(s), develop alternative solutions and recommend the best solution for the situation"*
> *Barbara A. Carkenord*

- What are the types of the requirements?
- How to categories the requirement?
- Is it really a requirement? It could be an assumption, dependency, project task, etc.
- What is the importance of this requirement (prioritization)? Urgent, critical, nice to have, etc.
- Does the business really need this requirement?
- Are there any alternative solutions?

3. **Document and present the requirements:** requirements can be presented as a BRD arti-fact, workflow diagram, use case, prototype, etc.

1. Elicit requirements

Requirements Elicitation is the process of capturing the stakeholders' needs and defining their goals and objectives from the project. In this process you will be capturing ALL kinds of requirements to be then analyzed in the next process.

- In Project Management (PMBOK), this process is called Collect Requirements
- In Business Analysis (BABOK), this process is called Requirements Elicitation
- In Lean Six Sigma, this process is called Define the Voice Of Customer – VOC *(Chapter-7)*

Needs vs. Requirements

Before we talk about the various requirements gathering techniques, we need to clearly understand the difference between a requirement and a need.

Requirement is defined by the International Institute of Business Analysis (IIBA) as a condition or capability required by a stakeholder to solve a problem or achieve an objective, while a need is a high-level representation of the requirement needed. The need is the end result or goal or objective.

Let's take a look at these examples:

Need	Requirement

▪ Build a house	▪ The house shall have 3 bedrooms
	   ○ 2 small bedrooms
	   ○ 1 Master bedroom
	       • The master room shall have 2 windows
	▪ The house shall have a backyard
	▪ The house shall be 3 levels
	▪ The floors shall be wood
	   ○ The wood color shall be dark brown

▪ Get a BA job	▪ Analyst shall read the "3D Business Analyst" Book ▪ Analyst shall create resume ▪ Analyst shall get ready for interviews
▪ Building a website	▪ The website shall have a log in request ▪ The website shall be available 24/7 ▪ The website shall have a navigation cursor

So the requirements are what need to be done in order to achieve the need or goal. Also you can look at it from the other side, a need is high level requirement that is segregated into a lower-level, more detailed requirements.

In the first example (Build a house), note how requirements can be segregated into more detailed requirements to define all the client's needs.

- What is the first thing you will be doing when you are on-boarded to a new project?
- What documents do you need to start eliciting requirements?
- Give me a preview of what your first week will be like when you are hired as a BA?

Now, what do you need to start with the requirements elicitation process? (see figure 2-10)
1. The project charter – it includes the customer's high-level requirements (needs)
2. The stakeholders register – so that you know who is who and doing what
3. Read any historical materials and artifacts from similar previous projects, which will help you to better grasp the project requirements
4. Review the organization's As-Is process flows and blueprints to be able to understand their current systems and how they interact with each other, this process is called Business Modeling

- Business Modeling is a very useful process because most of the projects in any organization are enhancement projects rather than building new systems from scratch. This will allow you to understand the organization's systems.
- Ask your project manager to provide you with the documents you need.

Requirements elicitation techniques

There are several techniques that you will be using to gather requirements from different subject matter experts (SME's). The PBMOK and BABOK define the requirements gathering tools and techniques as follows:

- How do you elicit requirements?
- How do you create the requirements document?

1. Interviews

By talking to the SME's *one-on-one*, you can get them to explain exactly what their requirements are and understand the whole concept of the project. It is a very effective way to know how they will use the product or service the project is creating.

Interviews can be conducted via e-mails, phone calls or face to face meetings.

2. Focus groups

Focus groups are similar to interviews, but they involve a specific set of stakeholders and SME's into the session instead of one-on-one interviews. It is another way to get a group of people to discuss their requirements with each other and try to find a solution. With the focus groups technique, you can get the business to tell you requirements that they might not have thought of by themselves. (This is elicitation)

- Always remember that you should go one more step beyond collecting requirements to eliciting requirements, this means that you keep asking questions and dig deeper until you get a comprehensive set of requirements that thoroughly describes the system you are creating.

3. JAD sessions (Joint Application Development)

JAD sessions are a series of structured collaborative workshops, where a facilitator (BA) leads the group through brainstorming requirements together. It brings together business area people (users) and IT (Information Technology) professionals in a highly focused workshop.
JAD participants typically include:
- Facilitator-facilitates discussions, enforces rules
- End users – 3 to 5, attend all sessions
- Developers – 2 or 3, present to provide technical clarity
- Tie Breaker – senior manager
- Observers – 2 or 3, do not speak
- Subject Matter Experts – limited number to help understand the business and technology

The workshop follows a detailed agenda in order to guarantee that all uncertainties between parties are covered and to help prevent any miscommunications.
In the end, this process will result in a new information system that is feasible and appealing to both the designers and end users.

Advantages of JAD sessions:
- Help bring experts together giving them a chance to share their views, understand views of others, and develop the sense of project ownership
- Reduce time for requirements collection
- Improve the quality of the final product by focusing on the up-front portion of the development lifecycle
- Reduce the likelihood of errors that are expensive to correct later on
- Misunderstandings and issues can get reconciled all at once because all of the stakeholders are working together to define requirements

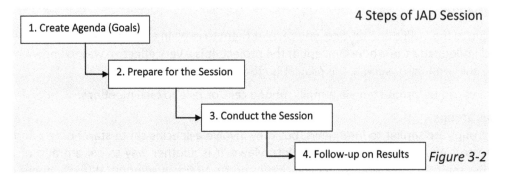

Figure 3-2

How do you plan (prepare) for a JAD session?
- Select the participants – consult your PM
- Schedule when everyone can make the appointment
- Distribute agendas before session
- Make surroundings as comfortable as possible (for example, you can bring snacks or coffee)
- Book enough time to discuss all topics in the agenda

4. Questionnaires and Surveys

Questionnaires and surveys are tools that allow you to get requirements from a bigger group of people, like the department's staff or end users. The questions are created in a way as to elicit requirements from the respondents, such as:
- What do you want the new software to do?
- Does the current software you are using satisfy your needs? Why, why not?
- And you can ask more detailed questions about the current system performance, interface, etc.

When you develop the questionnaires and surveys list, make sure the questions are specific and not confusing because in this tool you cannot interact with your audiences and you do not get the chance to have follow-up questions to get clarifications.

5. Observation

Also known as *Job Shadowing*. Sometimes you will face a situation where the customers do not know what their requirements are. Job shadowing is to watch a potential user of the product during their day-to-day tasks and participate in their work to help identify the product's requirements and see things from the customer's point of view.

6. Prototype

A Prototype is a quick implementation of an incomplete but functional application, which is a very effective way to communicate with clients when they are not clear about the requirements they are expecting. It helps the customer get an actual feel or hands-on experience of how the system will behave and work, since the interactions with a prototype can enable the client to better understand the requirements of the desired system.

Then the missing functionality can be easily identified and added. Also, the experience of coding a prototype is very useful for developers when developing the final system resulting in reducing the cost of development and producing a more reliable system.

Where do we find requirements?

- Domain Experts: also known as Subject Matter Experts, they are people who are very knowledgeable and work in the area of the system that is being built
- Users: they are people who will actually use the system
- Existing processes and programs: performing gap analysis between the current state of the system and the future state to identify the business needs
- Similar solutions or competing programs can be a great source

Requirements Elicitation Tips

- The choice of the requirements elicitation technique is left to you
- You will specify the techniques you will be using in the RMP (see RMP template in chapter 10)
- Before session:
  - Make sure to invite the appropriate stakeholders to your sessions (consult your PM)
  - Read through all available documentation, it is a key to understanding what the current state is, why a need for change has emerged, what could be improved, and so on
  - Have a look at reusable parts within the existing IT landscape that may be applicable in the future solution, as we mentioned earlier it's quite common that the new solution is not brand new
  - Research the business domain you are working on to familiarize yourself with domain knowledge and context. This will make you more comfortable in communicating with stakeholders and will increase your professional value
  - Explore the best practices for the domain you are working on, discuss them with the stakeholders and identify the ones that could be applied
  - When researching, make sure your reference material is current. There is nothing more embarrassing then finding out you spent days reading material that is out of date and no longer relevant
- During session:
  - Do not hesitate to ask about acronyms and terms used in the conversation, some of these terms and acronyms are industry wide while many others are simply internal jargon used by stakeholders to simplify their communication
  - Identify stakeholders and their roles in the daily routine
  - Make a note of what services (business applications and special tools) are used to support their business activities and what triggers them
  - Learn who does what, when and why
  - Pay attention to the rules used throughout daily activities, what they imply and why (policy or other documents). These rules might require further investigation to check whether they will be used in the new solution
  - See the requirements management cheat sheets for the interview questions guide
- After session:
  - Follow-up with stakeholders on the action items
  - Document what you gathered so far and send to stakeholders for review and feedback
  - Start requirements analysis process (discussed next)
- What can you do when key participants do not show up?
  - Ask for representatives to act on their behalf, if available
  - Conduct session as planned, follow-up after with the missing participant
  - Reschedule to meet their schedule, check if they want to meet remotely (teleconference)
  - Redefine the meeting agenda to be achievable with only those present
  - Consider an alternative interviewing technique
  - If nothing is working, escalate to PM or sponsors

2. Analyze Requirements

After you elicit all the requirements, your role as a BA is to analyze these requirements. As each requirement is analyzed, it generally leads to further questions; this requires the BA to probe further until all relevant issues are cleared.

- Requirement analysis is an iterative process, which means that you will need to meet the business again and again until you get what we call a "GOOD or SMART REQUIREMENT"

Requirements Analysis means performing the following tasks to make sure the requirements you have captured are feasible, valid, compatible, and consistent:
- Requirements categorization, what are the types of requirements?
- Requirements prioritization according to their level of urgency
- Define assumptions and constraints
- Verify requirements
- What is a good requirement?
- Who is the requirement owner?
- Validate requirements
- Is it really a requirement?
- Resolving competing requirements
- Root-Cause Analysis
  - ○ Fishbone diagram (Ishikawa diagram)
  - ○ 5 whys technique

Define assumptions, dependencies and constraints

Now that you have a large list of unorganized requirements, you need to extract the "not a re-quirement" from this list. It could be an assumption, dependency, project task, communication, etc. – anything else, but not a development requirement.

Let's elaborate with a simple example, if you have a requirement that says:
- *System A shall send a daily feed to System B*

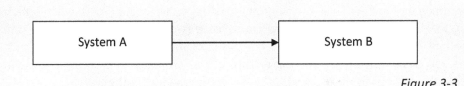

Figure 3-3

Sending a daily feed from A to B, this sounds like a requirement, ok good let's just document it and send it to the business for approval. HOLD ON!! Now what you did is not analysis, you just documented whatever the business said and that's it. This is a very common mistake business analysts fall in to, they forget that they are called analysts because they are supposed to ANALYZE what they elicit and document it in a requirements form, and always remember that your job is not to just host the meeting and write meeting minutes and call it requirements.

Here is how we can analyze this simple requirement example, by asking the following questions:

1. **What is the current (As-Is) status? Is this a new functionality?** Because the current status could be that system A already sends a daily feed to system B which will make this not a requirement, it is business as usual (BAU). It is preferred to add this as an assumption to make sure it is documented somewhere in the document and not missed, but at the same time it is not listed as a development requirement. Developers could get confused and think there is a development effort needed here which will affect their time and cost estimates and will have further impacts on the project plan. See how small mistakes in analyzing the requirement can lead to further impacts? *This is called Gap Analysis: the difference between current and future status.*

2. **How will this feed be sent? Manually or automatically?** What we need to understand from this question is whether the daily feed will be sent automatically by the system, then this will make it a requirement. It could be that the feed will be sent by the staff using System A, that will make it "not a requirement", in this case it is a dependency.

3. **What is the trigger for system A to send the feed?** The trigger will be a dependency

4. **Is this requirement In Scope for the project?** It is your job to explain to the business that out of scope requirements will be rejected.

5. **In what format should the feed be sent?** You will need to add a requirement specifying the format.

6. **Do you have a template of that feed? Can I have a look at it?**

7. **If yes, Is this template changing?**

8. **What are the success criteria?** You will need to add the success criteria in your BRD for the testing team to create the test cases

9. **Who is the requirement owner?** The owner will need to review and approve the requirement

10. **And so on....**

- These questions are real time project questions that you can use as a guide in your elicitation sessions.

Did you notice how a simple requirement may need a good amount of analysis work from your side? Again, you are an analyst, you are here to ask questions and understand the requirement and how it will fit into the overall system. The business SME's will only focus on their small piece, it is your job to be able to see the big picture of the project and be able to integrate all the requirements together to make sure they don't contradict each other.

How would requirements contradict each other?

Let's look at the same example, so we have two requirements that say:

1. *System A shall send a daily feed to system B*
2. *System B shall be secured to not accept any feed (or any input)*

If you look at these two requirements now it is obvious that they contradict each other, but it gets more complex when you have a list of 700+ requirements for 40 systems interfacing with each other. That's why defining the types of requirements and categorizing requirements can come in handy.

Before we move on to the types of requirements, let's have few more examples on analyzing a requirement because this is one of the most crucial skills for a BA:

- *The quality department shall be provided training on using the new application*

First question to ask yourself:
- Is it a development requirement?
- Is it something the developers will need to write a code to create?

(If you don't know the answer, you can ask the business SME or Owner or the developers themselves. Remember that it is OK to ask but it is not OK not assume wrong)

If your answer is YES, then this is a requirement and you need to continue with your analysis like in the previous example.

If the answer is NO, it is not a development requirement, then your analysis will take a different path. In that case you will need to do the following:

1. This will be added in your BRD as an assumption, to make sure it is document-ed somewhere in the requirements document and not missed

  - Make sure you ALWAYS document everything in the requirements docu-ment; you don't want to miss anything discussed in the elicitation sessions.

2. Inform the PM to add it to project tasks

3. Know who or which department is providing the training and communicate the training needs with them

- *System A shall be loaded with the necessary data*

This is a very common situation for a business analyst; usually when the business SME's are discussing the requirements, they do not know how the requirement should be written. Note that we only accept unambiguous specific requirements, so when you are in an elicitation session, you will hear many similar statements like "load necessary data" or "to do some activity in the appropriate time" or "some system shall retire soon". These are all examples of ambiguous requirements that need you to start asking questions to clarify and specify them, such as:

1. What are the necessary data? and add this to the requirements
2. How do you want the data to be loaded? What format?
3. How many times? Is it a onetime thing?
4. What do you mean by appropriate time? I need something more specific like a date or specific period of time
5. When is the system retiring?

If some of the questions do not have an immediate answer you can assign it as "TBD" and then follow-up until you get answers.

Let's try a more complex example:

- *You are conducting an elicitation session to gather requirements for an update to "System A" and you don't know yet much information about this system. Before you start asking about their requirements, you need to understand the overall function of that system and other systems impacted to be able to ask the right questions. Here is how I would start:*

    1. Can you please give me an overview on system A, what is it and what does it do?
    2. What are the inputs and outputs to the system? When? How often?
    3. What are the systems interfacing with the system?
    4. What do we want to achieve?
    5. And so on!

Then draw a high level process flow or blueprint, if it's not already available. You can even diagram it on paper during the session. (Process flows discussed in chapter 5)

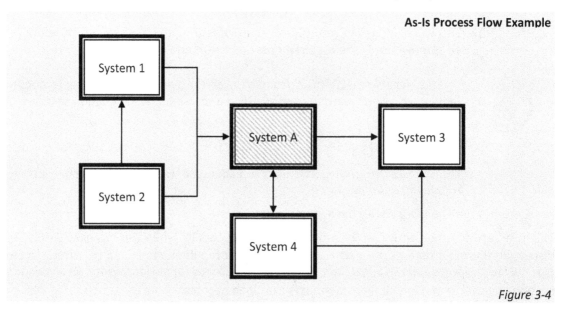

As-Is Process Flow Example

Figure 3-4

Always use visual representations. Business people are not technical; visual representations are very effective and help them understand their needs.

- Make sure you capture the current process flow (As-Is) and use it in the elicitations sessions.

Now you have a better understanding on System A and the other systems it's impacting, now it's time to start gathering the requirements and asking questions, such as:

1. What do we need to upgrade in system A?

2. How would this update affect systems 1, 2, 3 and 4?

3. Since system A sends feeds to systems 3 and 4, does this mean they will need to be updated as well?

4. After the upgrade, will system A still need to send feeds to systems 3 and 4?

5. If not, do we need to communicate with these systems to make sure they are ready for the update?

6. Capture the Future process flow (To-Be)

7. Perform Gap analysis process

Types of requirements

There are two broad types of requirement:

1. High-level requirements (Business objectives, goals or needs) – they describe top level goals and overall systemic features and are more abstract in nature. Also called Business Requirements.
2. Low-level (detailed) requirements – describe individual components within the system and how they operate, detail rather than overview, rudimentary functions rather than complex overall ones.

Categorizing requirements

Unfortunately, we do not elicit requirements in a logical order. Business stakeholders, in most cases, do not award us their requirements straightforward in an organized linear fashion. They usually discuss solutions and we elicit their requirements from disordered discussions. That is why it is important to categorize the gathered requirements: to be able to keep track of them and make them easier to define, document, double check, and review.

Let's say for example, the business stakeholders only want to review the business requirements that are independent of technology or the technical stakeholders want to review functional and technical requirements. Categorizing the requirements will make it easier to navigate through the gathered requirements instead of having the stakeholders reviewing the entire package and search for items they are looking for. Categorizing requirements is also an effective way to make sure no requirements are missed.

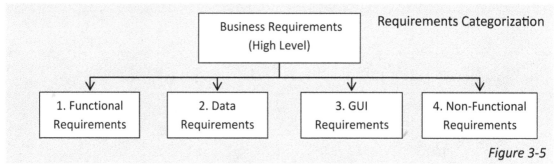

Figure 3-5

In figure 3-5, the business requirements describe the high level goals and objectives of the stakeholders. The business requirements are then segregated into lower level requirements to describe the system in a more detailed way.

There is no one RIGHT categorization system that works for all organizations. Any system will work if used properly, so regardless of how you categorize and present requirements, you must let your viewers know where to find things. That's why a table of contents for requirements is essential.

The four main requirements categories are:

1. Functional requirements
2. Data requirements
3. Graphical User Interface (GUI) requirements
4. Non-functional requirements

---

1. Functional requirements

"Functional requirement describes the behavior and information that the solution will manage. They describe capabilities the system will be able to perform in terms of behaviors or operations – a specific system action or response." (BABOK V2.0, 2008)

This means that functional requirements describe the functionality of the product or what tasks the solution must perform, such as:

- Login to a system
- Checkout functionality
- Print functionality

2. Data requirements

Data requirements can be described as the conceptual data elements or information needs, such as:

- The comments field shall be 7 characters
- The password shall contain a number, uppercase and symbol
- The username shall be not less than 8 characters

3. Graphical User Interface requirements (GUI requirements)

GUI requirement is pronounced (*gou-wee*) in most American organizations; however it is pronounced G-U-I (letters) in Europe and Asia. GUI requirements are the user interface design considerations, or you can basically think of *GouWee* requirements as anything you see on the screen and it involves defining the various parameters and screen controls.

Let's see the examples below:

Radio Button	○ Yes ◉ No ○ May be
Text Box or Comments Field	Username: [ ]
Check Box	☐ Sales ☐ Marketing ☐ Finance ☑ IT ☐ Select All

4. Non-functional requirements

It might get a little confusing to define the non-functional requirements, so let's take it step by step. A non-functional requirement is "any requirement that is not functional". However, this definition is not sufficient enough because if we take data requirements for example, they are clearly not functional requirements but neither are they non-functional requirements. Same thing for GUI requirements – they are neither functional nor non-functional requirements.

Then let's define non-functional requirements as any requirements that cannot be categorized into functional, data or GUI requirements.

At this point all we know about non-functional requirements is that:
- They are requirements
- They are not functional, data or GUI requirements

The International Institute of Business Analysis defined non-functional requirements as follows:
- "Non-functional requirements are the quality of service requirements that are most often used to describe some of the attributes of the system or system environment. These requirements are constraints on the solution" (BABOK v1.6, 2006)
- "Non-functional requirements capture conditions that do not directly relate to the behavior or functionality of the solution, but rather describe environmental conditions under which the solution must remain effective or qualities that the system must have. They are also known as quality or supplementary requirements" (BABOK V2.0, 2008)

That being said, we can summarize that non-functional requirements describe how fast, how efficiently, how safely, etc. a particular task is carried out by a particular system.

- Easy way to identify non-functional requirements is: if you can't categorize a requirement into functional, data or GUI then it's a non-functional require-ment.
- The thing to really worry about is missing a requirement not miss-categoriz-ing a requirement.

So what is a requirement that is not functional, data or GUI? This could be any of the following:
- Usability – is this application useable by any system?
- Security – who can access the system? Shall external users be provided access to the system?
- Scalability – expansion or upgrade requirements. For example, the initial intent for Gmail is to send and receive emails. Nowadays you can create your own profile page and connect to friends and network through Google+. How many users did Gmail have originally? And look at it now! This is scalability; it means that it is able to accom-modate higher number of users. Do you think the system built by Google to support thousands of users is the same one used now to support millions?
- Availability – describes the accessibility of the system e.g. the system shall be available on weekdays from 9 am to 5pm, or the system shall be available 24/7
- Reliability – how reliable is the system? Will it crash?
- Interoperability – can this system work if other competing system is in place? If the

system can work in harmony with other systems, this is called Interoperability

- Extensibility – the ability to extend the application services or products. Can you expand the system services?
- Maintainability – is the system easy to maintain or it is hard coded (e.g., do we have the ability to go back and fix the bugs)? Can you maintain the functionality within the system?
- Portability – is this application portable? Can you just plug it and install it wherever you want?
- Business rule – organizational policies, guidelines, and controls
- Quality – it is the ability to conform with the business requirements
- Resilience – the ability to come back to its original shape
- Recovery – is it easy to recover after the system is crashed? Can you recover the data?
- Etc!

- Note that non-functional requirements tend to be the 'ilities" of the system such as: availability, accessibility, etc.

A final point – each organization has its own categorizing system that is appropriate for their business – and like we agreed earlier, there is no one right categorizing system. Any logical system will work if used properly.

In very rare cases, if your organization does not have a consistent categorization system, create your own system and present it to the PMO. REMEMBER, any system is better than none.

Let's look at the following real life example of how users explain their requirements in a "whole bunch of things" format and how we categorize them:

"Hey, this system is awful: it takes more than 15 minutes to load an order! What we want is a system that can retrieve the client details as soon as the operator enters the client name and ID number – oh and we will also need the operator to be able to validate these data with the client – hmmm and due to the government privacy regulations we need to save the data for 5 years."

Now, you will need to extract the requirements from this paragraph and categorize them into a more structured system. Here is how you should analyze this information:

1. A <u>goal</u> is to reduce time taken to load an order from 15 minutes, to what? (you need to ask)

2. A <u>goal</u> to maintain compliance with government regulations (what are these regulations? You need to ask to see what other regulations we might have to comply with)

3. A <u>non-functional (security) requirement</u> to provide the operator access to the system (who else can use this process? Just the operator? All operators or just a specific staff?)

4. A <u>data requirement</u> to create two fields to enter clients name and ID number (how long is the field? You need to ask)

5. A <u>non-functional requirement</u> to retrieve the client data

6. A <u>functional requirement</u> to validate customer data

7. A <u>non-functional requirement</u> to save the client data for 5 years (non-functional because data is saved automatically without function from users)

8. When do you want this system to be available for your team to use? 7 days a week? 24 hours? Any days off? How about vacations? Etc! **(Availability Requirements)**

9. How many times do you expect the team will be using the system per day? How many is the staff using it? **(Capacity Requirements)**

10. When you say "as soon as" the operator enters the clients name and ID number, do you really mean instantly because this will have a huge impact on the cost of the solution or is there an acceptable period of time like 2 seconds? **(Performance Requirements)**

11. How reliable do you need the system to be? Do you want the system to be available 100% of the time? Again, this will have a huge cost impact or it is acceptable if the system goes down for no more than 1 day per year) **(Reliability Requirements)**

12. And so on!

Prioritizing requirements

Prioritizing requirements is the process of representing the priority of a given requirement relative to all other requirements and the business goals of the project.

Prioritization can be as follows:

- Critical requirement – is essential for acceptance of the solution

- Important requirement – is important to the effectiveness or efficiency of the system and/or its functionality. Lack of inclusion may affect customer or user satisfaction, but the release will not be delayed due to lack of this feature

- Nice to have requirement – is useful but no significant revenue or customer satisfaction impact may be expected if the requirement is not included

This system can be used or any other prioritization system in your organization; just like the categorization system.

Verify requirements (What are Good Requirements?)

- What is a good requirement?
- What is a SMART requirement?

A Good Requirement Should Be:

- **Complete** – they describe the criteria very well
- **Correct** – they are accurate and true
- **Feasible** – they can be accomplished and don't contradict each other
- **Necessary** – they are truly needed for the system to function properly and they are really what the client wants
- **Prioritized** –because not all parts of the system can be applied the same time and it's important to be able to distinguish "absolutely necessary" from "nice to have"
- **Unambiguous** – they are clear and cannot be misinterpreted
- **Verifiable** – can be observed and tested

SMART Requirement
Specific. Measurable. Achievable. Realistic. Traceable.

SEE INSPECTION CHECKLIST TEMPLATE IN CHAPTER 8

Root-Cause Analysis

There are many root-cause analysis tools. In this chapter we will be discussing the Fishbone diagram and 5 Whys technique. They are a powerful tools used to uncover the root cause of a problem and help the team push beyond symptoms.

Fishbone diagram

It is a structured method to guide a team through a problem-solving process to discover the root cause of a problem. It provides a pictorial display of a list in which you identify and organize possible causes or problems.

Fishbone diagram is also known as Ishikawa or Cause and Effect diagram

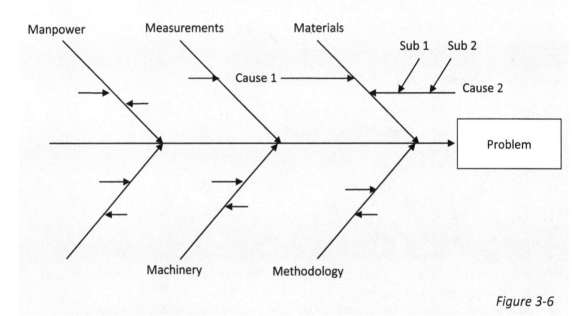

Figure 3-6

How to use the Fishbone diagram
1. Identify the undesirable effect or problem and write it at the head of the fishbone
   - *Let's say for example the problem is: Delayed Deployment*
2. Assign the major categories for causes (Typical categories includes the 6 M's: Manpower, Materials, Measurements, Methodology, Machinery, Mother Nature (environment))
   - *Let's assign category 1 for Materials*
3. Now use brainstorming techniques with the team to define more detailed causes. Walk through each category and ask "Why" each major cause happens (5 Whys technique explained next)
   - *Cause 1 will be: testing software not delivered on time*
     - *Why? (or Which is caused by)*
   - *Supplier did not meet our schedule*
     - *Why?*

- *The project schedule was not correct*
  - ○ *Why?*
- *The need date was determined incorrectly*
  - ○ *Why?*
- *Procurement did not understand priority*
  - ○ *Why?*
- *Lack of communication (**ROOT CAUSE**)*

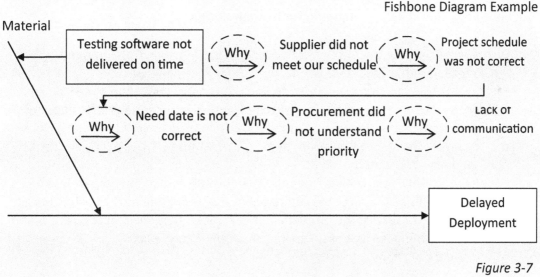

Fishbone Diagram Example

Figure 3-7

4. Continue until all problems have been traced to a root cause
5. Discuss the diagram with the team for completeness and present it to the business for final review
6. Identify the most critical root causes and develop an action plan

- The 80/20 rule: 80% of problems can be attributed to 20% of the causes.
- Also known as Pareto rule

5 Whys technique

You can use the 5 Whys technique in the root cause analysis to prevent the team from being satisfied by superficial solutions that will not fix the actual problem in the long run. This technique is also a useful tool in your requirements elicitation sessions to help you understand the need of a specific requirement.

Note that you do not always have to use 5 whys, it is just to imply that you need to dig deep to get the root cause. In some cases you may reach a root cause after two or three whys and in other cases you may find yourself needing to dig deeper to 6 or 7 whys. You can stop whenever the team feels they have reached a potential cause that they can act on.

- The Analyze phase defines the detailed user requirements to a level of detail sufficient for systems design to proceed
- The requirements at the end of this phase need to be measurable, testable, and relate to the high business requirements identified in the project charter (traceable)

Requirements Analysis Tips

- Discover the need of the business rather than invention: what is your need? What are your requirements?
- Facts rather than opinions: you need to find out the facts not someone's opinion.
- Questions rather than answers: one of the biggest misconceptions about business analysis is that a lot of people think the BA is supposed to invent the solution or will provide answers to the business problems. The business analyst discovers the solution but does not invent it
- "What" and "Why" rather than how: the "what is needed and why" part is your job, focus on understanding the requirements and asking the right questions to identify the root cause of the problem. The technical team, developers, testers and architects are the ones that are responsible for the "how" part.
- Ask the right questions

---

3. Document and Present Requirements

Documenting and presenting requirements is the third step in the requirements management process. After you elicit all the requirements and analyze them, you will have a list of organized requirements and well structured data on the project that you need to document and present to the business for review and signoff.

These requirements and data can be presented in any of the following ways and formats:
- Impact Assessment
- Requirements Management Plan (RMP)
- Business Requirements Document (BRD)
- Functional Requirements Document (FRD)
- As-Is and To-Be Process Flows (Also referred to as Current and Future States)
- Requirements Traceability Matrix (RTM)
- Process Modeling
- Use Cases
- Graphs
- PowerPoint presentations
- Etc.

- Think of this step as the output of the business analysis process or as the business analyst's products.

Requirements Management Plan (RMP)

The RMP document describes the approach that will be used for eliciting, analyzing, documenting, communicating and maintaining the requirements throughout the life of the project. The goal of the requirements management plan is to establish a baseline for development, and to ensure plans, work products, and activities are consistent with the solution requirements.

Think of the requirements management plan as the contract between you and the project manager, where it governs the business analysis work from end-to-end and the project scope. Also in the RMP you will identify the inputs provided to you to do your work and what outputs are expected from you. Your estimated work hours needed to deliver, these BA products will be used by the project manager in the project schedule and resources estimates. (See the life of a project diagram, figure 2-10)

Inputs could be:
- Project charter
- Solution blueprint
- Preliminary project plan
- Existing training material
- Existing modeling diagrams
- Existing use cases
- Historical project documentation

Outputs could be:
- Requirements management plan
- Business requirements document
- As-Is process flows
- To-be process flows
- Gap analysis
- Use cases
- Business process impact analysis
- Requirements traceability matrix

Requirements Traceability Matrix

The purpose of the requirements traceability matrix is to link the high level and detailed business requirements, use cases, functional requirements and test cases.

During your requirements elicitation, it is very common to find that one high level requirement will lead to more refined requirements and clarifications. The traceability matrix is used to help you keep track of all the high level requirements segregated to more detailed ones, then to functional and technical requirements, then to test cases.

In the functional design phase, all business requirements should have their corresponding technical requirements on how they will be developed. In the testing phase, all technical requirements segregated from the business requirements should have their test cases and success/fail criteria. This way you will guarantee that no requirement is missed.

The matrix is used throughout the project. It is created in the requirements elicitation phase and updated in the analyze, design and test phases.

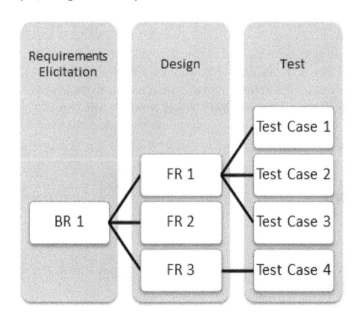

Figure 3-8

Business Requirements Document (BRD)

The BRD artifact is a form used to present and document the business needs and the target end users, and to describe why these needs exist. The high level requirements and project charter are inputs to the BRD. (See the life of a project diagram, figure 2-10)

The BRD should answer the question, "What capabilities are needed to solve the problem or achieve the objective?".

Process Modeling using UML Diagrams

UML is a modeling language which puts together several diagrammatic views that can be used at any stage of the software development life cycle to specify, visualize, modify, construct and document the system artifacts.

Types of UML Diagrams:
- Sequence diagram
- Class diagram
- Activity diagram (Swimlane or cross-functional diagram)
- Component diagram
- Deployment diagram
- Collaboration diagram
- Decomposition diagram
- Use Case diagram

The UML diagrams will be explained thoroughly in chapter 5.

Requirements Documentation Tips

- Be precise and concise in your writing
- Make reference to all sources that were used in the preparation of your documents
- Ensure that your references are available to other stakeholders and members of your project team
- Documenting the requirements in a structured way saves a lot of the organization's effort and time for any consecutive project to enhance the delivered solution
- Add notes in your documents to make it easy for readers to find their information (e.g., see requirement #3, see assumption #2, etc.)
- Always run the spelling and grammar checker after each update
- Have someone proofread your documents (peer review)
- Make your documents CLEAN (same font, size, consistent, etc.)

User Stories

User stories are another method for describing the behavior of a system. It is a technique that was developed as part of extreme programming and agile methodologies, in which requirements ("user stories") are written as one or two sentences in the everyday or business language of the user. Each user story describes a meaningful interaction with the system from a user's point of view. They are collected on index cards, so that they must stay very brief to fit on the card. The intent of the user stories method is not to document system behavior, but to elicit conversations about it. This is in keeping with the Agile Manifesto's preference for collaboration, interaction, and working software over documentation, negotiation, and tools. As such, the user stories are not numbered, are not typed up, and are frequently discarded when the work is complete.

User stories are ideally written using a suggested sentence format of:

As a (role), I can (perform some action), so that (some goal is achieved)

For example,

- As an operator, I can check the status of a member, so that I can know if I should expect payment or not.
- A member can request a new ID card to be mailed to their home.

The format, like everything else about user stories, is not strict. In some organizations the user stories are written in a real story format, such as:

Joe is a customer with a user account on the organization's member portal. Joe navigates to the home page because he would like to download his membership information. On the home page, Joe selects "Member" tab and types his username and password then clicks the "login" button. When he is logged in he will select his membership information and click on the download button on the bottom left side. The selected membership information is then downloaded to Joe's computer in a PDF format.

A few things to note:

- The roles do not necessarily have to correspond to a human. An internal or external system or process can play a role.
- User stories should be:
    - **I**ndependent of each other (as much as possible)
    - **N**egotiable – They are deliberately kept abstract and avoid details on purpose.
    - **V**aluable to users – the outcome of each story should be of some value to the user(s)
    - **E**stimatable – they need to be small enough that a rough order of magnitude can be established
    - **S**mall – complex or compound stories about lengthy, hard to describe interactions need to be broken up into smaller stories
    - **T**estable – there needs to be a clear way to know if a user story ended successfully or not

The acronym INVEST can help remember these attributes of good user stories. Same as good requirements, these are the characteristics of good user stories

Things to remember when creating a user story

- Make sure to obtain a complete set of user stories, to ensure that the requirements are complete and correct, in order to define a product that will be suitable for use by the business. In particular you must ensure:
    - o   All roles have been identified
    - o   All interactions the users will perform have been identified
    - o   The goals of each story is known
- Make sure the entire ecosystem of the project is considered with regard to user stories. Stories should include:
    - o   The primary usage of the system (workflows, user interactions, interfaces between systems)
    - o   Secondary uses of the system (administration, management, monitoring, reporting)
    - o   Visible security concerns (what is and is not authorized)

Step-by-Step

1. From the scope document, write up the user stories you envision as you understand them.

    a. Identify the users and the roles they will play

    b. Identify the actions the users will take in their various roles

    c. Identify the goals of the actions

    d. Identify scenarios where each action should work and should not work

    e. Make sure to consider:

        o Roles that might not be people (external systems that trigger actions in this system)
        o How the system will be administered
        o How the system will be monitored
        o How the system will be reported
        o How the system will be secured

2. Look for stories that need to be split or joined – check that the stories are Independent, Negotiable, Valuable, Estimatable, Small, and Testable.

3. Arrange a review of the user stories by the business.

    a. If you believe it would be helpful, provide them a copy of this document so they can get background on what we are trying to accomplish.

4. Exchange the user stories documentation back and forth between yourself and the business, adding, correcting, or amplifying as needed.

5. Make sure the requirements in the BRD cross-reference the user stories that support them.

6. When the BRD is complete and the user stories are documented, review both simultaneously and obtain signoff for both.

II. Requirements Communication

The rationale of adding the communication area in this chapter is that as requirements are elicited, analyzed and documented, they need to be communicated to the concerned stakeholders. Requirements communication is an important skill for a 3D business analyst, where he/she will be working to bring different stakeholders and implementers of the project to a common understanding of the requirements to get their buy-in on the final solution.

To understand how to effectively communicate with stakeholders, you need to be familiar with the <u>6</u> communication concepts below:

1. Plan Communications

It is the process of planning the communication needs throughout the project, such as:

- Who needs what information? (example, Sr. management need project status report)
- In what format? (Status meeting, email, phone, etc.)
- When will they need it? (Wednesdays, 9 am)
- How it will be given to them? By whom? (Status will be presented by the BA)
- How frequently? (Weekly)

- Inaccurate communication planning might lead to project risks such as communicating sensitive information to the wrong audience which could impact the project plan.

2. Communication Model

The communication model is a basic mock-up of how communication takes place between individuals, shown in figure 3-9 below:

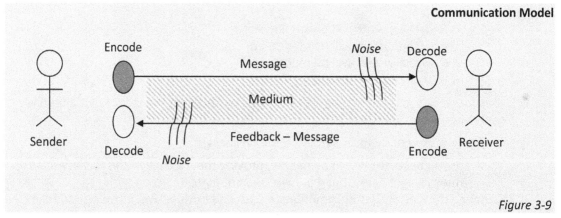

Figure 3-9

The key components of the model are:

- Sender and receiver
- Medium: method utilized to pass on the message
- Noise: any sort of interference that could affect transmitting and understanding a

message. Such as, language, distance, noisy surroundings, lack of information, lack of education, etc. These are also called *communication blockers*
- Encode: is to convert information and data into a message that is understood by others
- Decode: is to convert the message back into meaningful information or data
- Message and feedback: a feedback message is sent back to the sender to confirm it was interpreted correctly

- Make it a habit to give feedback of how you understood the information and requirements you are eliciting. This is called Effective Listening.
- Use lines like "So what I'm hearing is that you want the system to….", "let me make sure I got this right", and so on.

3. Effective Communication

It means providing information:
- In the right time
- Right format
- Right impact

When you are the sender, you need to make sure to encode your message carefully, determine which communication method to use (meeting, phone, email, etc.) to send it and confirm the message is correctly understood by asking for feedback.

4. Efficient Communication

Efficient communication means providing only the information that is needed to each stakeholder.

5. Communication Method

Various methods are used to communicate information with stakeholders; they can be broadly categorized into:
- Interactive communication: this is the most efficient way to exchange information between two or more people. Interactive communication includes meetings, phone calls, conversations, etc.
- Push communication: this is a one way stream (no feedback expected) sent to someone who needs to know specific information. This method does not confirm the message has reached the receiver and understood correctly. Push communication includes reports, letters, memos, etc.
- Pull communication: used for large volume of information, where all information is uploaded to a centralized location and interested recipients pull information as needed. Pull communication includes e-learning, SharePoint, Intranet sites, etc.

6. Communication Types

Information can be communicated in several ways:
- Formal or informal
- Written or verbal

Requirements Communication Tips

- Practice speaking with stakeholders using domain specific language, terms and acronyms. The more you get comfortable with these items, the more effective communication you will have. The stakeholders will get the feeling that you are an insider and are working on their side
- Understand the existing state well enough to be able to articulate the pathway to the target state
- Present the current state, why the need has emerged, what could be improved and so on
- Your communication should be aimed to outlining a new business context in comparison to its existing state
- Emphasize the value of best practices because they will support the expected benefits and provide additional long term value to stakeholders
- Plan your communication well and adjust your speaking style to match your audience

1. Elicit Requirements

- **Requirements elicitation** is the process of capturing the stakeholders' needs and defining their goals and objectives from the project
- A **requirement** is a condition or capability required by a stakeholder to solve a problem or achieve an objective
- A **need** is a high-level representation of the requirement needed. The need is the end result or goal or objective
- **What do you need to start with the requirements elicitation process?**
  - Project Charter
  - Stakeholders register
  - Read any historical materials and artifacts from similar previous projects
  - Business Modeling: review the organization's As-Is process flows and blueprints

❖ ELICITATION TECHNIQUES

- **Interviews** is talking to the SME's *one-on-one*, to get them to explain exactly their requirements
- **Focus groups** are similar to interviews, but they involve a specific set of stakeholders and SME's into the session instead of one-on-one interviews
- **JAD sessions (Joint Application Development)** are a series of structured collaborative workshops, where a facilitator (BA) leads the group through brainstorming requirements together. It brings together business area people (users) and IT professionals in a highly focused workshop

  JAD participants typically include:
  - Facilitator–facilitates discussions, enforces rules
  - End users – 3 to 5, attend all sessions
  - Developers – 2 or 3, present to provide technical clarity
  - Tie Breaker – senior manager
  - Observers – 2 or 3, do not speak
  - Subject Matter Experts (SME's)

- **Questionnaires and surveys** are tools that allow you to get requirements from a bigger group of people, like the department's staff or end users

- **Observation technique** is to watch a potential user of the product during their day-to-day tasks and participate in their work to help identify the product's requirements and see things from the customer's point of view. Aka Job Shadowing
- A **Prototype** is a quick implementation of an incomplete but functional application

  Where do we find requirements?
  - Domain Experts: also known as Subject Matter Experts, they are people who are very knowledgeable and work in the area of the system that is being built
  - Users: they are people who will actually use the system
  - Existing processes and programs: performing gap analysis between the current state of the system and the future state to identify the business needs
  - Similar solutions or competing programs can be a great source

❖ INTERVIEW QUESTIONS GUIDE

- **To the business SME's:**
  - Can you give me an overview on the system?
  - Can you walk me through the process?
  - Does this represent your needs?
  - Did we miss anything?
  - Any possible alternative scenario?
  - Are all possible impacts considered?

- **To the project manager:**
  - Are the requirements in scope?
  - What is the approval strategy?
  - Do we know whom to speak to about the problem?
  - Do we have any schedule, budget or risk constraints?

- **To the developers:**
  - Can you develop these requirements?
  - Do we have any conflicting requirements?
  - What is the impact of these requirements on the technical components?

- **To the testers:**
  - Can these requirements be tested?
  - Do you have any testing issues?

2. Analyze Requirements

- **Define assumptions, dependencies and constraints**
- **Categorize requirements** to be able to keep track of them and make them easier to define, document, double check, and review
  - The 4 main requirements categories are:
  - i. **Functional requirements**: they describe the behavior and information that the solution will manage. They describe a specific action or response to the system
  - ii. **Data requirements**: they are described as the conceptual data elements or information needs
  - iii. **GUI Requirements (GouWee)**: they are the user interface design considerations. (anything that is seen on a the screen, such as radio button, text box and check box)
  - iv. **Non-functional requirements**: they are requirements that cannot be categorized into functional, data, or GUI requirements. This could be any of the following:
    - Usability
    - Security
    - Scalability
    - Availability
    - Reliability
    - Interoperability
    - Extensibility
    - Maintainability
    - Portability
    - Business rule
    - Resilience
    - Recovery
- **Prioritizing requirements** according to the business goals of the project into critical, important and nice to have requirements
- **Verify requirements** is the process to ensure the requirements are good and SMART

  What is a good requirement?
  - **Complete** – they describe the criteria very well
  - **Correct** – they are accurate and true
  - **Feasible** – they can be accomplished and don't contradict each other
  - **Necessary** – they are truly needed for the system to function properly and they are really what the client wants
  - **Prioritized** –because not all parts of the system can be applied the same time and it's important to be able to distinguish "absolutely necessary" from "nice to have"
  - **Unambiguous** – they are clear and cannot be misinterpreted
  - **Verifiable** – can be observed and tested

  What is a SMART requirement?
  - Specific
  - Realistic
  - Measureable
  - Traceable
  - Achievable

3. Document Requirements

- Requirements and data can be presented in any of the following ways and formats:
  - Requirements Management Plan (RMP), describes the approach that will be used for eliciting, analyzing, documenting, communicating and maintaining the requirements throughout the life of the project
  - Business Requirements Document (BRD), is a form used to present and document the business needs and the target end users, and to describe why these needs exist
  - Requirements Traceability Matrix (RTM), to link the high level and detailed business requirements, use cases, functional requirements and test cases
  - Functional Requirements Document (FRD), is a formal statement of application's functional requirements
  - As-Is and To-Be Process Flows (Also referred to as Current and Future States)
  - Impact Assessment
  - Process Modeling
  - Use Cases
  - Graphs
  - PowerPoint presentations

  - ❖ DOCUMENTATION TIPS

- Be precise and concise in your writing
- Make reference to all sources that were used in the preparation of your documents
- Ensure that your references are available to other stakeholders and members of your project team
- Documenting the requirements in a structured way saves a lot of the organization's effort and time for any consecutive project to enhance the delivered solution
- Add notes in your documents to make it easy for readers to find their information (e.g., see requirement #3, see assumption #2, etc.)
- Always run the spelling and grammar checker after each update
- Have someone proofread your documents (peer review)
- Make your documents CLEAN (same font, size, consistent, etc.)

WALK ME THROUGH A BRD CONTENTS!!!

1. BRD name (e.g. Business requirements for Project)
2. BRD number (e.g. version 1.0)
3. Business Case
4. Introduction:
   - 4.1. Project Overview
   - 4.2. Project goals and objectives
   - 4.3. Analysis performed to develop requirements
   - 4.4. Approach/methodology
   - 4.5. Risks
   - 4.6. Assumptions
   - 4.7. Dependencies
5. Project scope
   - 5.1. In-scope
   - 5.2. Out-of-scope
   - 5.3. Constraints
6. Business processes and workflows
   - 6.1. Current process flow (As-Is)
   - 6.2. Future process flow (To-be)
   - 6.3. Gap Analysis
7. User stories
8. Use case

> Walk me through a Use Case template!!
>   - Use case name
>   - Use case overview
>   - Actors
>   - Flow of events
>   - Special requirements
>   - Preconditions
>   - Post conditions
>   - Use case diagram
>   - Use case matrix

9. Requirements matrix
   - Business req.
   - GUI req.
   - Security
   - Functional req.
   - Non-functional
   - Other requirements........
   - Data req.
   - Training
10. Success criteria
11. References
12. Glossary

TEMPLATES CHANGE FROM ONE ORGANIZATION TO ANOTHER

User Stories

- User stories are another method for describing the behavior of a system
- It is a technique that was developed as part of extreme programming and agile methodologies, in which requirements ("user stories") are written as one or two sentences in the everyday or business language of the user.
- Each user story describes a meaningful interaction with the system from a user's point of view

Requirements Communication

1. **Plan communication** is the process of planning the communication needs throughout the project

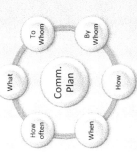

2. **Effective communication** means providing information: in the right time, right format and right impact

3. **Efficient communication** means providing only the information that is needed to each stakeholder

4. **Communication method:** there are various methods can be utilized to communicate information with stakeholders; they can be broadly categorized into:
   - Interactive communication, such as: meetings, phone calls, conversations, etc.
   - Push communication, such as: reports, letters, etc.
   - Pull communication, such as: SharePoint, e-learning, etc.

5. **Communication types:** information can be communicated in several ways. (formal, informal, written and verbal)

4

SDLC Methodologies

Software Development Life Cycle (SDLC)

The Software Development Life Cycle (SDLC) – aka systems development life cycle – is a framework used in project management to describe the stages involved in building information system projects in a very organized manner from the initiate and plan phases through the system design and code development and to the testing and deployment phases.

The SDLC is a structured, integrated approach that is characterized by a sequence of phases in which each phase is incomplete until the appropriate deliverables are produced. There are several SDLC models that have been created to guide the processes involved, such as:

- Waterfall methodology (traditional SDLC model)
- Rapid Application Development (RAD)
- Rational Unified Process (RUP)
- Agile
- Scrum (a form of agile)

Some methodologies work better for specific types of projects and fit the organization structure better than others. Regardless of the type of model management decides is the best for their application development, in the final analysis, the most important factor for the success of a project shall be how closely the chosen methodology was followed.

Generic SDLC components:

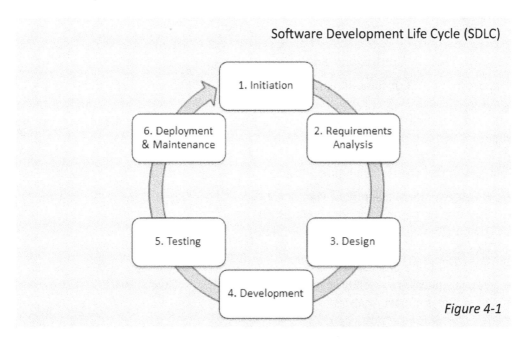

Figure 4-1

1. Initiation

The initiation phase is where the "Business Case" and "Project Charter" are created and presented to the sponsor for approval.

The following tasks take place in the project initiation phase:
- Concept Proposal – talking to the business sponsor to know the high level requirements and the overall concept of the project
- System Scope or boundaries – to know from the sponsor what the scope is – what does he want and the budget for that.
- Cost/Benefit Analysis – to know how much it is going to cost, and decide if an application should be built in-house, purchased or outsourced. Information from the "IT Manager" may be useful to understand the technology piece of the project, or discussed with some vendors.
- Feasibility study – to check if the project is feasible or not and if the project should get the "Go ahead"
- Risk Analysis – indentify, analyze and prioritize all the project risks
- Stakeholder Analysis
- Resources on-boarding

Key Outputs of initiation phase: (see figure 2-10)
- Kick-off meeting
- Project charter
- Impact analysis (or impact assessment)
- Stakeholder register
- Issues and risks

2. Requirements gathering and analysis

Eliciting, analyzing and documenting requirements is the primary role of a business analyst, as discussed in chapter 3. The purpose of this phase is to document, verify, analyze, prioritize, validate and baseline the system requirements to provide the foundation for the design, development and test phases.

Keys outputs of this phase: (see figure 2-10)
- Requirements Management Plan (RMP)
- Business Requirements Document (BRD)
- Functional Requirements Document (FRD)
- Use Cases
- As-Is and To-be process flows
- Requirements Traceability Matrix (RTM)
- Update the Impact Analysis

3. Design and Technical Architecture

The design phase involves the interpretation of the system requirements identified in the requirements analysis phase to a unified system design that describes the characteristics of the application to be built.

Keys outputs of this phase:

- Conceptual Architecture
- Functional design specification
- Technical design specification
- Update the requirement traceability matrix

4. Development

The development phase is where the actual code is written by developers. The programming is done based on the documentation provided to them from the previous phases. In the development phase, the design specifications are transformed into a complete and integrated application.

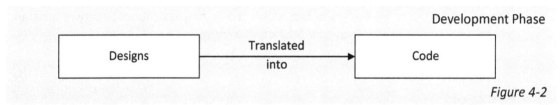

Figure 4-2

The business analyst's role is minimal in this phase. In implementation phase, the BA role is to explain the gathered requirements to the developers and answer queries about the system raised by the developers.

Main tasks in the implementations phase:
- Build the components of the solution
- Review code
- Conduct unit test and integrate all individually developed and tested components into an executable application
- Transition of the application to the test team
- Create the implementation backout plan, to assist the project to manage and monitor implementation effectively and plan actions needed if the associated change or release fails.

Different programming languages like C, C++, Java are used for coding. The most appropriate programming language is chosen with respect to the type of application.

5. Testing

In the test phase, the various components of the developed application are integrated and tested to validate that all identified requirements have been satisfied prior to deployment. The testing team prepares and executes the functional test to ensure each application meets the business and system requirements. The system is then tested as a whole to make sure that all applications work together as a complete solution.

Various testing stages:

1. Unit Testing: this is usually done by the developers who have coded the unit to ensure requirements have been satisfied
2. Integration Testing: this is done by the QA team and/or the BA to test that the integration of the units is working fine
3. System Testing: is done by the QA team or the BA to see whether the system is working as a whole or not
4. Regression Testing: is done to test whether the current parts and the new development are synchronized and there is no impact on any other system
5. User Acceptance Testing (UAT): is covered by the end users in order to test that the requirements given for the system are in line with the developed application
6. Stress and/or Load Testing: is done by the technical team to test whether the system can sustain heavy load and usage
7. Incremental Integration Testing: checks for bugs, which may be encountered when a module has been integrated into the existing modules
8. Smoke Testing: it is the battery of test which checks the basic functionality of program. If fails then the program is not sent for further testing

Keys outputs of this phase:

- Test plan
- Test cases
- Test results
- Performance reports

- In some organizations, the BA role involves testing tasks like creating and reviewing test cases, identifying UAT scenarios which would be suitable to test and mapping use cases into UAT documents. In other organizations, the BA role is minimal in the testing phase and he/she is present to support the testing team and to explain the system to them.

6. Deployment and Maintenance

Deployment starts after the code is appropriately tested, approved for release and distributed into a production environment. Maintaining and enhancing the software to cope with newly discovered problems or new requirements, the software should be developed to accommodate changes that could happen during the post implementation period.

- Development environment is where the application is built by the developers
- Testing environment (QA) is where the application has been validated by the testing team
- Production environment is where the actual end user uses the system (which is live)

- Describe the business analyst role in the different phases of SDLC.

Overview of the Project Phases, Deliverables, & Team Structure

SDLC Phase	Description	Main role
Initiation	All necessary analysis is undertaken to determine if the project is worth the investment or not	PM & BA
Requirements Gathering and analysis	Elicit, analyze and document the requirements for the application being developed and create requirements documents, use cases, & UML diagrams	BA
Design	Create software design	System Architects
Implementation	Code the application	Developers
Testing	Test the application to ensure its compliance/agreements with the requirements	QA, Developers, & BA
Deployment	Release the application in production environment to the users	Release Mgmt Team, Deployment Team, System Admin, PM, Dev, QA, & BA

Various SDLC methodologies:

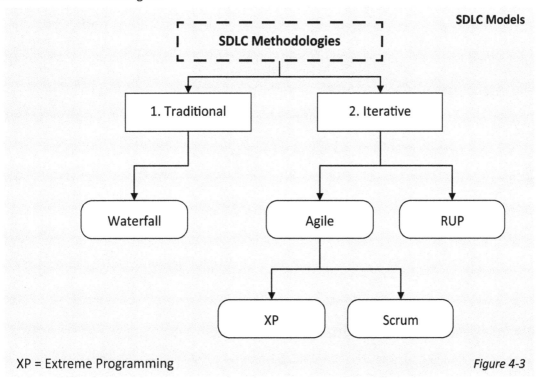

XP = Extreme Programming   *Figure 4-3*

1. Traditional Model

Traditional model is a linear sequential lifecycle framework like Waterfall. In the sequential model, each phase must be completed in its entirety before the next phase can begin and a review takes place at the end of each phase to determine if the project is on the right path, and whether or not to continue or discard the project.

The linear structure of this model makes it simple to understand and use, and easy to manage due to its rigidity where each phase has specific deliverables and a review.

2. Iterative Model

The Iterative approach is also known as Incremental or Progressive lifecycle model. In this model, multiple development lifecycles take place making the model a "multi-waterfall", where cycles are divided up into smaller and more easily managed iterations; each pass through a full lifecycle loop. A functioning system is produced in iteration 1 and built upon during each iteration thereafter, which grows incrementally from iteration to iteration to become the final system. (Like a snow ball)

The iterative framework generates functioning software quickly and during early stages of the lifecycle. Also, it is more flexible to change in scope or requirements and easier to test and debug since it has small iterations.

Waterfall Methodology

The waterfall is a *sequential* software development methodology, in which activities or phases are seen as falling steadily from top to bottom (like a waterfall) through the phases of initiation, requirements, design, development, testing and deployment as shown in figure 4-4 below:

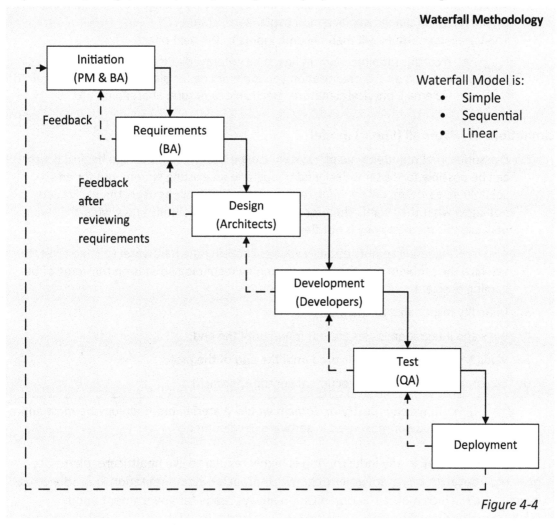

Figure 4-4

The Waterfall is a traditional SDLC approach that assumes phases of a project can be completed **sequentially** which means one phase leads to the next phase. It is a **linear** model, can only go in one direction and it states that when a phase is performed, it is frozen and signed off in strict order. This makes it **simple** and easy to explain to users and team members.

In this methodology, stages and activities are well defined and verification sign-off is performed after each stage to ensure detection of errors as early as possible.

The linear structure of activities has some important consequences:

- In order to clearly identify the end of a phase and beginning of the others, a certification (formal sign-off) is needed at the end of each phase
- This means that each phase must have a predefined output that can be evaluated and certified
- This certified output is called "baseline" and can only be changed or modified in a controlled manner (change management explained in chapter 2)
- The baselined outputs will then become inputs to the next phase

- A certification mechanism has to be employed at the end of each phase. Depending on the organization you are working for, sign-offs could be acquired via email, physical signature, electronic signature, SharePoint, etc.

Limitations of Waterfall (linear) model

1. It assumes that requirements of a system can be frozen before design begins, which can be possible for systems designed to upgrade an existing system, but for an absolutely new system, determining requirements is difficult as users themselves do not know what they want. Therefore, users need to absolutely know what they want because this methodology is not flexible for changes.

2. Also freezing requirements usually requires choosing the hardware, so large projects will face the problem that they have to employ technology that is on the verge of becoming obsolete.

3. Difficulty responding to changes.

4. Bugs and integration issues are not found until the end.

5. Value to customer is not delivered until the end of the project.

6. Excessive documentation (document centric approach)

- In which industry or domain would Waterfall methodology be most appropriate or most used in software development?

Waterfall works well in any industry that is highly regulated like healthcare, pharmaceutical, etc., because it is a document centric approach – documentation is produced at every stage – which makes the organization always ready for government audit.

It also works well for smaller projects or projects where requirements are very well understood.

- Since the BA's main role is in the initiation and requirements phases, the BA will be idle in the design, development, and test phases. Same thing for architects, developers, and testers; they are idle in other phases outside their role. This means, resources are not utilized to their fullest potential in the Waterfall model.

Rational Unified Process (RUP)

The Rational Unified Process is an ***iterative*** software development approach that provides a disciplined process to assigning tasks and responsibilities within a development organization. Its goal is to ensure the development of high quality software that meets the needs of its end-users, within an estimated schedule and budget by implementing a project management structure to SDLC that has phases and iterations – each having its templates and guidelines.

What is an iteration? Iteration means the act of repeating a complete development loop with the aim of approaching a desired goal or target result. Each repetition of the process is called an "iteration" and the results of one iteration are used as a starting point of the next iteration.

In the project management chapter, we defined five phases of the Project Life Cycle (PLC); in RUP there are four PLC phases:

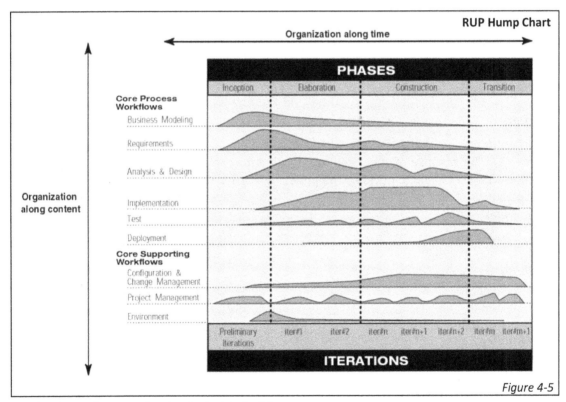

Figure 4-5

1. **Inception** – understand what to build
2. **Elaboration** – understand how to build it
3. **Construction** – the actual building phase
4. **Transition** – transitioning the product to the end user community and get stakeholders acceptance

Each phase has one key objective and milestone at the end that denotes the objective being accomplished.

> In RUP, one phase begins before the preceding phase is completely done or closed. Therefore, "Elaboration" starts before the "Inception" phase is completed and the "construction" phase starts before the "Elaboration" phase is signed-off, and so on.
>
> Example:
>
> Let's say that there are 10 requirements that need to be implemented:
>
> - 1st step: 5 would be in Initiation and the other 5 requirements are not yet started
> - 2nd step: 5 requirements will be in Elaboration phase and another 3 would be in Inception and 2 are not yet started
> - 3rd step: 5 would be in Construction and 3 would be in Elaboration and 2 in Initiation and so on.

 ▪ In RUP, there are <u>4</u> PLC phases, <u>6</u> engineering disciplines and <u>3</u> supporting disciplines.

a) <u>RUP PLC phases</u>

1. Inception

The Inception phase in RUP is very similar to the "Initiation" phase in project management (chapter 2). The purpose of the inception phase is to explore the project with the business stakeholders (clients) and to decide if the project is worth the investment or not.

Key deliverables:

- Business Case
- Project Charter
- Project Scope
- Project Plan
- Estimate overall cost and schedule
- Risk Analysis
- High level requirements and Use Cases

The BA has a minor role in this phase creating high level requirements and may not be involved this early in the project.

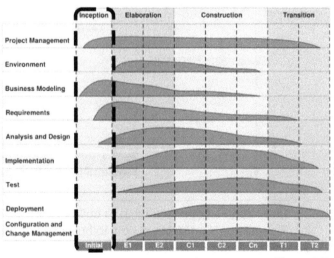

Figure 4-6

2. Elaboration

The purpose of the elaboration phase is to elicit and analyze the business needs and to stabilize the design of the system. The project starts to take shape in this phase.

Key activities and deliverables:
- Segregate high level requirements and Use Cases into detailed and analyzed requirements
- Requirements baseline
- UML diagrams
- Design baseline
- Change management
- Produce a comprehensive plan for the next phases

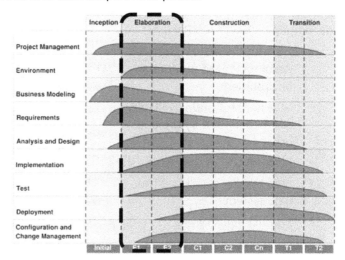

As you can see in figure 4-7, the elaboration phase is usually broken down into two or more iterations depending on the size and nature of the project.

Figure 4-7

Also note that even though the Elaboration phase is mainly for requirements, analysis and design tasks; implementation, testing and deployment tasks start in this phase.

The majority of the BA role falls in the Elaboration phase.

3. Construction

The construction phase is where the actual coding is done. All the project components and features are developed, integrated and tested.

Key deliverables:
- System coding
- Produce the first external release
- Test plan
- Test cases
- Iteration plan detailing next iterations
- Transition strategy to be used in the next phase

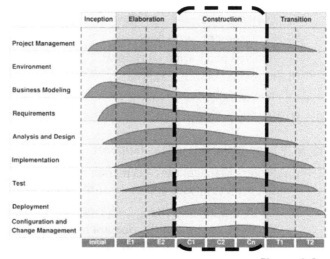

Figure 4-8

The BA role in this phase is to continue working on the requirements, analysis and design tasks (as shown in figure 4-8) and to answer questions raised by developers and testing team.

4. Transition

The transition phase is simply the phase where the system/product developed is put in the hands of the client and the stakeholders formal acceptance is acquired.

Key activities and deliverables:

- Transfer the system from the development to production environment
- Making the system available and understood by the end users
- Perform UAT at the client's site
- Beta testing to validate the new system
- Product delivery
- Project documentation
- Training of users and maintenance team

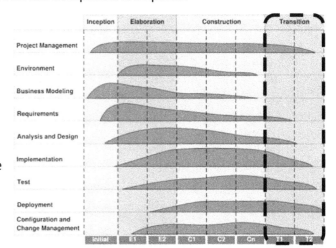

Figure 4-9

The BA role in the transition phase is to train end users on the new system and perform UAT testing at the client site.

b) <u>RUP Engineering Disciplines</u> (Core Process Workflows)

They are, to some extent, similar to the Waterfall methodology phases.
   a) Business Modeling workflow
   b) Requirements workflow
   c) Analysis and design workflow
   d) Implementation workflow
   e) Test workflow
   f) Deployment workflow

c) <u>RUP Supporting Disciplines</u> (Supporting Workflows)

   a) Project Management – is managing, executing and controlling the project throughout the project phases and make sure it meets the defined goals in the project charter

   b) Configuration and change management – configuration management is managing the different versions of the documents created throughout the project. Change management is explained in chapter 2

   c) Environment – the purpose of the environment workflow is to provide the organization with tools, templates, guidelines and processes needed to support the team – it is basically a step-by-step process to describe how to implement a project in an organization

Spiral Methodology

The Spiral model is an enhancement of the Waterfall methodology; it extends the Waterfall by introducing the perception of prototyping. The Spiral methodology is generally chosen over Waterfall for large and complicated projects.

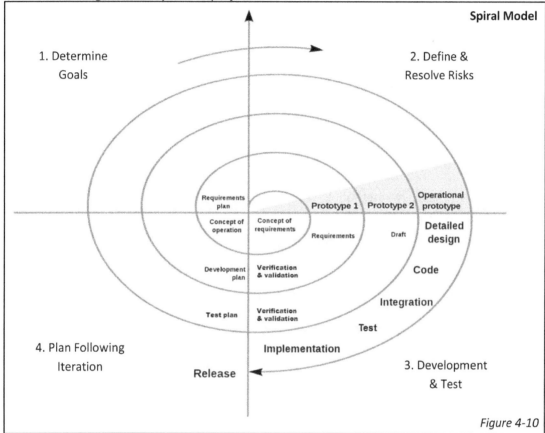

Figure 4-10

The Spiral model allows the system to be delivered incrementally according to a prioritized set of features presenting a prototype to the system at the end of each cycle until the system is completed.

The Spiral model process

1. Each cycle begins with the determination of goals and objectives for that specific pro-totype (cycle) and different alternatives of achieving the defined goals

2. Identify risks or uncertainties anticipated and evaluate previously defined alternatives based on the project objectives

3. Perform development and testing activities to resolve determined risks

4. Plan for the next prototype which is bigger and more detailed

Strengths of the Spiral model

1. More flexible to changes, where it is an incremental improvement on the waterfall methodology

2. Risks are identified earlier in the project so that schedule and budget estimates become more realistic as work progresses

3. High amount of risk analysis (risk driven approach)

4. Can incorporate other methodologies within the spiral framework

Weaknesses of the Spiral model

1. Applied differently for each application

2. Due to too many releases, there is a risk of not meeting budget or schedule

3. Does not work well for smaller projects

4. Project success is highly dependent on the risk analysis phase which requires highly specific expertise

- The Spiral methodology follows the concept **"Build a little, test a little"**, where it builds and tests working versions of the software to learn and acquire information and gradually evolve to the final design.

Prototyping

Prototyping is a quick implementation of an incomplete but functioning application to help the customer get the actual feel or hands-on experience on how the system will behave and work, since the interactions with prototype can enable the client to better understand the requirements of the desired system.

The rationale of prototyping is to create a demonstrable result as early as possible and present it to the business and end users to get their feedback, then refining that system until it is accepted by the client. Also, the experience of developing a prototype is very useful for developers when creating the final system, which results in reducing the cost of development and more reliable system.

Rapid Application Development (RAD)

The RAD model was created to fill in the need to deliver systems very fast (50 – 70 days) with some compromises. It involves development of systems in a considerably lesser time period by using workshops or focus groups to gather requirements, prototyping and re-using software components.

This method may not be advisable if creating an application that is going to be used a stand-alone system, but such development cycles help you when you are aiming at development of a system that is going to be part of an entire system.

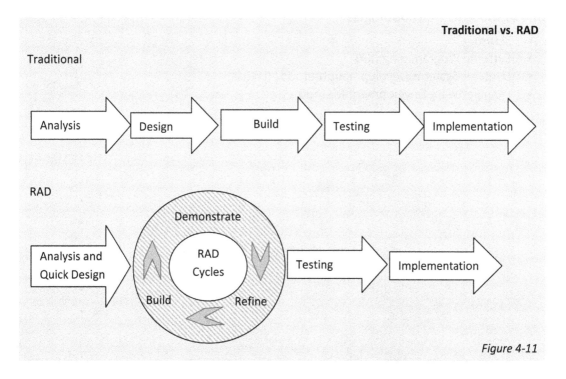

Figure 4-11

Agile Software Development

Agile is a group of iterative and incremental methodologies used in project management to support project managers building software applications that are unpredictable in nature. It focuses on user involvement through teams and workshops with business analysts and developers.

The rationale of agile methods is to minimize the risk by developing applications in short time boxes called iterations. The iterations typically last one to four weeks and each iteration is a project of its own. It includes:

1. Planning	4. Coding
2. Requirements Analysis	5. Testing
3. Design	6. Deployment

In agile, value is achieved faster as releases arrive at the customer more frequently in the form of sprints (iterations). At the end of each sprint, an increment of work is presented by the development team.

In conclusion, agile models deliver the biggest and most comprehensive applications/systems more quickly with small number of rules. Best practices are used that are easy to employ which makes it a good model for environments that change steadily.

Some of the agile methodologies:

- Scrum
- Extreme Programming (XP)
- Dynamic Systems Development Methods (DSDM)
- Lean Software Development Method

Scrum Methodology

Scrum methodology is a member of the agile family that inherits its iterative philosophy of developing applications in short time boxed iterations called **Sprints**. Therefore, scrum can be defined as an iterative, incremental structure that is used in project management that focuses on user involvement through teams and workshops with business analysts and developers.

A key principle of scrum is it can accommodate requirements changes at any point of the project allowing customers to change their minds about their needs and what they need.

- In waterfall, changing requirements is called a change request; while in scrum it is often called requirements churn.

Scrum methodology brings all people to the same room enabling the creation of self organized teams and verbal communication takes place across all team members and disciplines that are involved in the project.

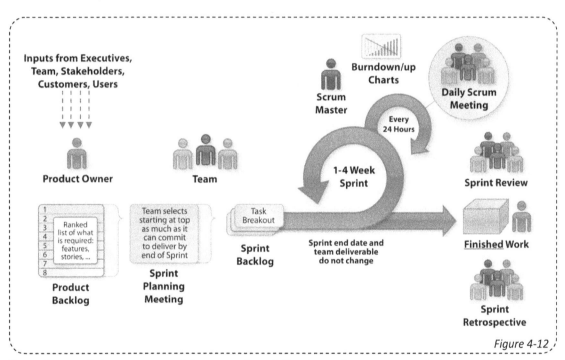

Figure 4-12

To understand the scrum model we need to define its unique process skeleton which contains three broad categories:

1. Roles	2. Artifacts	3. Ceremonies/Meetings

1. Scrum Roles (Chicken and Pig)

> ### The Chicken and Pig Story
>
> Once upon a time there were friends, a pig and chicken, who decided to start their business. They opened a restaurant and it was time to create their menu, so the pig asked the chicken, "What kind of food should we serve?" The chicken suggested, "Let's serve ham and eggs".
>
> The moral of the story is that pigs are the ones committed to the project in the scrum process because they are the ones with their "bacon" on the line performing the actual work of the project. (Scrum Master, the Team, and Product Owner)
>
> Chicken roles are not part of the actual scrum process, but must be taken into account. They are people for whom the software is being built. (Stakeholders, customers, functional managers)

The Pig roles are:

- *Product Owner* – is the voice of the customer and is accountable for creating and prioritizing the requirements or User Stories (customer-centric items) then adding them to the product backlog
- *Scrum Master* – represents the project manager role in other methodologies, who ensures the scrum practices and rules are followed and is accountable for facilitating the project to deliver its deliverables
- *Scrum Team (Cross-functional team)* – IT team typically consists of 5 – 9 people with cross-functional skills who do the actual work (analyze, design, develop, test, communication, documentation, etc.) to deliver the product. Scrum team can only be changed between sprints

Product Owner	Scrum Master
<ul><li>Responsible for maximizing the business value (ROI)</li><li>Only one person in charge</li><li>Accepts or rejects work</li><li>Helps define what work has been done</li><li>Knowledgeable, empowered and engaged</li></ul>	<ul><li>Responsible for facilitating the process</li><li>Helps build a self organized team</li><li>Removes impediments</li><li>Enforces rules</li><li>Servant leader</li><li>Empowering the team; not ordering and controlling</li><li>Acts as a bridge between the top management and the team</li></ul>

The Chicken roles are:

- *Managers* – they are people who will set up the environment for the product development organizations
- *Stakeholders* – people for whom the product is being built

2. Scrum Artifacts
- *Product Backlog* – a prioritized list of high level requirements and objectives of the project – can also be called "wish list"
- *Sprint Backlog* – a selected list of tasks that the team will commit to complete during the sprint. A sprint is typically from 1 to 4 weeks
- *Sprint Burn Down Chart* – it is a publicly displayed chart showing the remaining work (daily progress) in the sprint backlog

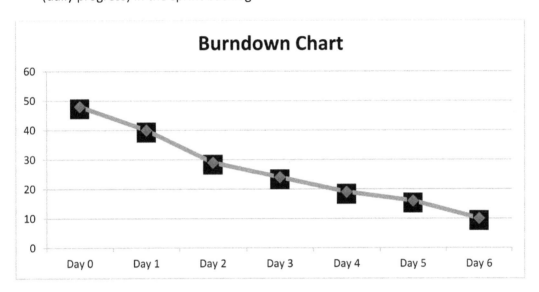

3. Scrum Ceremonies/Meetings
- *Daily Stand Up Meeting* – this is a daily 15 minute meeting between pigs and chickens to ask 3 questions:
    - I.   What did you do yesterday?
    - II. What is planned for today?
    - III. What obstacles are in your way?

In this meeting only pig roles (Scrum Master and the project team) are allowed to speak.

- *Sprint Planning Meeting* – this meeting occurs in the beginning of each sprint cycle (every 7 – 30 days) to discuss what is to be done in the upcoming sprint and create the sprint backlog. This meeting has an 8 hour limit
- *Sprint Review Meeting* – this meeting occurs at the end of each sprint to demonstrate the completed parts to the stakeholders; incomplete parts are not demonstrated. (4 hours limit)
- *Sprint Retrospective* – in this meeting all team members provide feedback on the past sprint and work on making continuous process improvements by asking two main questions:
    - I. What went well during this sprint?
    - II. What could be improved in the next sprint?

- What happens in each sprint?
- How do you plan for a sprint?

Now that we defined the different scrum roles, artifacts and ceremonies, let's see how does the scrum model works? *(See figure4-13)*

Life of a Scrum Project

1. Preparation phase: the project customers, end users and stakeholders provide their input to the product owner, who is the voice of customer, and creates the business case, scope and high level requirements (HLR). The initial product backlog is created.

2. Prioritize product backlog: The product owner will then prioritize the product backlog according to their importance to the business users. Items that add immediate and significant business value are bubbled up to the top.

3. Create sprint backlog: A sprint planning meeting is held by the team. In this meeting the product owner informs the team of the items in the product backlog that they want to complete. The team then determines how much of this they can commit to complete within a 30 days period and record this in a sprint backlog. During each sprint, the requirements are frozen and no one is allowed to change the sprint backlog.

4. A daily 15 minute scrum meeting is held to track progress using burn down charts.

5. Product increment: Every 30 days the team should present a potentially shippable product increment that provides value to the business. (release)

6. After a sprint is completed, the team demonstrates how to use the software.

7. Now that the sprint is completed and presented to the business, before starting a new sprint, a sprint retrospective meeting takes place to continuously improve the upcoming sprints.

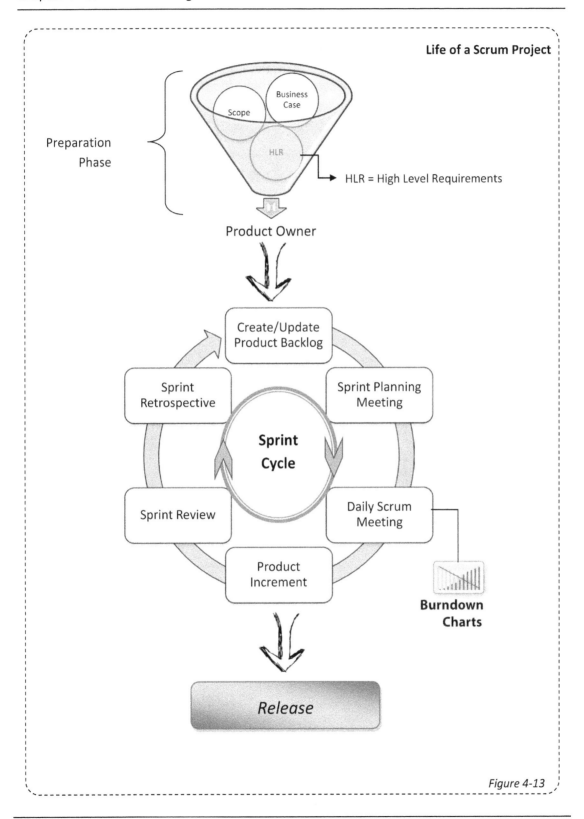

Figure 4-13

Strengths of scrum

- Scrum saves the project's time and money. Because there are no time consuming/wasting tasks, the team comes in and does their job right away. (e.g. no excessive documentation, like waterfall)
- Scrum is very useful for large projects where requirements are not very well understood.
- Like any other iterative agile methodology, it requires continuous feedback from the business which ensures the customer is satisfied with the end product.
- Due to short sprints (1-4 weeks) and constant feedback, it is more flexible to cope with changes.
- Daily meetings allow measuring the individual productivity, which leads to improving the overall team's productivity.
- Daily meetings also help identify and resolve issues well in advance.
- Scrum is a highly controlled process where its skeleton contains frequent updating of the work progress through various meetings – thus, there is a clear visibility of the project development.

Weaknesses of scrum

- Agile scrum is one of the leading causes of scope creep because unlike waterfall, the scope is not frozen or baselined and there is no definite end date to requirements gathering which tempts stakeholders to keep demanding new functionalities.
- Works well only with small teams.
- The risk of losing a team member during the project can have a huge negative impact on the project development.

- Remember the following keywords or terms:
    - Waterfall is a <u>document</u> centric oriented
    - Scrum is a <u>time</u> centric oriented
    - XP is a <u>code</u> centric oriented

Software Development Life Cycle (SLDC)

- SDLC is a framework used in project management to describe the stages involved in building information system projects in a very organized manner.

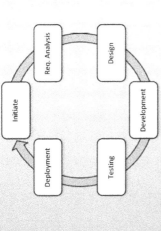

- There are various software development methodologies that follow these 6 steps; they just do it in different way.

1. The **initiation** phase is where the "Business Case" and "Project Charter" are created and presented to the sponsor for approval

2. **Requirements gathering and analysis:** the purpose of this phase is to document, verify, analyze, prioritize, validate and baseline the system requirements to provide the foundation for the design, development and test phases

3. The **design** phase involves the interpretation of the system requirements identified in the requirements analysis phase to a unified system design that describes the characteristics of the application to be built

4. The **development** phase is where the actual code is written by developers. The programming is done based on the documentation provided to them from the previous phases

5. In the **testing** phase, the various components of the developed application are integrated and tested to validate that all identified requirements have been satisfied prior to deployment

6. **Deployment** starts after the code is appropriately tested, approved for release and distributed into a production environment

- **Traditional model** is a linear sequential lifecycle framework, such as Waterfall. Each phase must be completed in its entirety before the next phase can begin and a review takes place at the end of each phase to determine if the project is on the right path

---

- In the **Iterative** model, multiple development lifecycles take place making the model a "multi-waterfall", where cycles are divided up into smaller and more easily managed iterations; each pass through a full lifecycle loop. A functioning system is produced in iteration 1 and built upon during each iteration thereafter, which grows incrementally from iteration to iteration to become the final system.

- **What is iteration?** Iteration means the act of repeating a complete development loop with the aim of approaching a desired goal or target result. Each repetition of the process is called an "iteration" and the results of one iteration are used as a starting point of the next iteration

SDLC Models

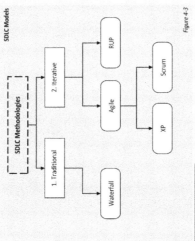

Figure 4-3

Prototyping

- Prototyping is a quick implementation of an incomplete but functioning application to help the customer get the actual feel or hands-on experience on how the system will behave and work.

- The rationale of prototyping is to create a demonstrable result as early as possible and present it to the business and end users to get their feedback.

Rapid Application Development (RAD)

The RAD model involves development of systems in a considerably lesser time period by using workshops or focus groups to gather requirements, prototyping and re-using software components.

Waterfall Methodology

The waterfall is a *sequential* software development methodology, in which activities or phases are seen as falling steadily from top to bottom (like a waterfall) through the phases of initiation, requirements, design, development, testing and deployment

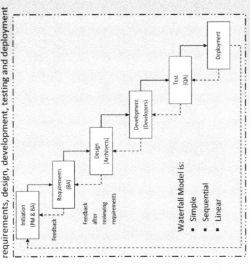

Waterfall Model is:
- Simple
- Sequential
- Linear

Waterfall works well in highly regulated industry like healthcare, pharmaceutical, etc. because it is a *document centric approach* that makes the organization always ready for government audit. It also works well for smaller projects or projects where requirements are very well understood

- **Limitations of waterfall (linear) model:**

1. It assumes that requirements of a system can be frozen before design begins, which can be possible for systems designed to upgrade an existing system, but for absolutely new system determining requirements is difficult as users themselves do not know what they want, therefore users need to absolutely know what they want.

2. Also freezing requirements usually requires choosing the hardware, so large projects will face the problem that they have to employ technology that is on the verge of becoming obsolete.

3. Difficulty responding to changes.

4. Bugs and integration issues are not found until the end.

5. Value to customer is not delivered until the end of the project.

6. Excessive documentation (document centric approach)

Rational Unified Process (RUP)

- It's an iterative software development framework that has been taken forward by Rational (part of IBM corporation)
  - ❖ RUP has four project life cycle phases

1. **Inception** – understand what to build, the purpose of the inception phase is to explore the project with the business stakeholders (clients) and to decide if the project is worth the investment or not

Deliverables: Business Case, Project Charter, Project Scope, Project Plan, High-level Requirements, Use Cases

2. **Elaboration** – understand how to build it, the purpose of the elaboration phase is to elicit and analyze the business needs and to stabilize the design of the system. The project starts to take shape in this phase.

Deliverables: Detailed Requirements, UML Diagrams, Design Baseline, Change Management

3. **Construction** – the actual building phase, the construction phase is where the actual coding is done. All the project components and features are developed, integrated and tested

Deliverables: System Coding, Test Plan, Test Cases, First external release

4. **Transition** – transitioning the product to the end user community and get stakeholders acceptance

Deliverables: UAT Testing, Beta Testing, Product Delivery, Project Documentation, Training

  - ❖ RUP 6 Engineering Disciplines:

1) *Business Modeling* – Initial modeling of business and scope formation
2) *Requirements* – gathering and communication of requirements
3) *Analysis and design* – analysis and formation of the solutions designs
4) *Implementation* – Implementing the solution
5) *Test* – testing the system as a whole and in units
6) *Deployment* – finally deploying the system at client site & going into production

  - ❖ RUP 3 Supporting Disciplines:

a) *Configuration and Change Management* – configuration of the versions of documents and code. Management of changes to requirements, solution and codes as required
b) *Project Management* – Planning, estimation, resourcing & overall managing the team & customers as part of the project
c) *Environment* - Ensuring that the project team is aware of all aspects and of the RUP implementation

Spiral Methodology

The Spiral model is an enhancement of the Waterfall methodology; it extends the Waterfall by introducing the perception of prototyping.

Strengths of the Spiral model

1. More flexible to changes, where it is an incremental improvement on the waterfall methodology
2. Risks are identified earlier in the project so that schedule and budget estimates become more realistic as work progresses
3. High amount of risk analysis (risk driven approach)
4. Can incorporate other methodologies within the spiral framework

Weaknesses of the Spiral model

1. Applied differently for each application
2. Due to too many releases, there is a risk of not meeting budget or schedule
3. Does not work well for smaller projects
4. Project success is highly dependent on the risk analysis phase which requires highly specific expertise

Agile

- Agile is a group of iterative and incremental methodologies used in project management to support project managers building software applications that are unpredictable in nature. It focuses on user involvement through teams and workshops with business analysts and developers.
- The rationale of agile methods is to minimize the risk by developing applications in short time boxes called iterations. The iterations typically last one to four weeks and each iteration is a project of its own. It includes:

1. Planning   2. Req. Analysis   3. Design
4. Coding   5. Testing   6. Deployment

- Agile models deliver the biggest and most comprehensive applications/systems more quickly with small number of rules. Best practices are used that are easy to employ which makes it a good model for environments that change steadily.
- Agile methodologies include:

  ○ Scrum   ○ XP   ○ DSDM

Scrum Methodology

- It is the most popular form of Agile
- Scrum is an iterative, incremental structure that is used in project management that focuses on user involvement through teams and workshops with business analysts and developers.
- Project is divided into short time boxed iterations called **Sprints**
- A sprint is typically from 1-4 weeks period

  ❖ SCRUM ROLES

(Pigs)

- Product Owner: is the voice of the customer and is accountable for creating and prioritizing the requirements or User Stories (customer-centric items) then adding them to the product backlog
- Scrum Master: ensures the scrum practices and rules are followed and is accountable for facilitating the project to deliver its deliverables
- Scrum Team (Cross-functional team): IT team typically consists of 5 – 9 people with cross-functional skills who do the actual work to deliver the product.

(Chickens)

- Managers – they are people who will set up the environment for the product development organizations
- Stakeholders – people for whom the product is being built

  ❖ SCRUM ARTIFACTS

- Product Backlog: a prioritized list of high level requirements
- Sprint Backlog: it is a selected list of tasks to be completed during a sprint
- Sprint Burn Down Chart: it is a daily progress chart of a sprint

  ❖ SCRUM MEETINGS

- Daily Stand Up Meeting – this is a daily 15 minute meeting between pigs and chickens to ask 3 questions:
  ○ What did you do yesterday?   ○ What is planned for today?
    ○ What obstacles are in your way?
- Sprint Planning Meeting: occurs in the beginning of each sprint cycle (every 7 – 30 days) to discuss what is to be done in the upcoming sprint and create the sprint backlog (*8 hours*)
- Sprint Review Meeting: occurs at the end of each sprint to demonstrate the completed parts to the stakeholders (4 hours)
- Sprint Retrospective: team members provide feedback on the past sprint by asking two main questions:
  ○ What went well during this sprint?
  ○ What could be improved in the next sprint?

5

Business Process Modeling

Unified Modeling Language (UML)

WHAT?

UML is a modeling language created by Rational Software in the 1990s and adopted by Object Management Group (OMG) in 1997. It puts together several diagrammatic views that can be used at any stage of the software development life cycle to specify, visualize, modify, construct and document the system artifacts.

UML is a set of standardized (Unified) diagrams, just like construction has front elevation, electrical diagram, floor plan, etc., UML offers different views of the same system.

WHY?

Why do we model? Well, developing a model for a software system prior to its development is as essential as having a blueprint for a large building construction, where it promotes better understanding of the requirements. Modeling is a very effective way for communication with stakeholders (customers, domain experts, designers, developers, etc.) and understanding the problem.

Like they say "A picture is worth a thousand words"

It allows the team to design and plan the system they are building before wasting any time coding the wrong design. Because in the long run, applications that are well planned and built with solid design are actually less time consuming to build, more flexible and easier to maintain than systems built by trial and error.

HOW?

How do we model? To answer this question we need to know the following:
- What are the different UML diagrams?
- Which team member is responsible of creating each diagram?
- What is each diagram used for?
- What are the tools to create UML diagrams?

UML diagrams are vital for business analysts, as they help them in getting the requirements validated and assessed where the diagrams add clarity to the functional specification documentation. Therefore they are widely used by business analysts to corroborate their requirements elicitation.

Types of UML Diagrams

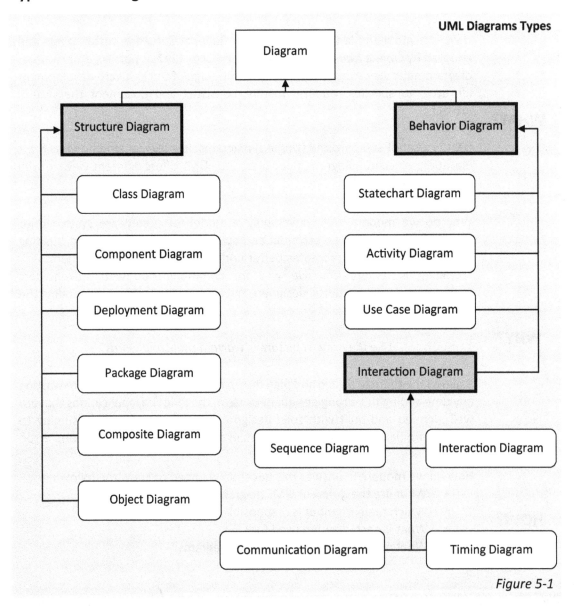

Figure 5-1

Out of these UML diagrams shown in Figure 5-1, Business Analysts worldwide would mostly use the Use Case Diagram, Activity Diagram and sometimes, Sequence and Class Diagrams. The majority of the rest of the UML diagrams are designed by the solution architect or designers. It is not essential that for any project all of the UML diagrams will have to be created. The UML diagrams are vital for a business analyst as they help him in getting the requirements validated and assessed.

1. Class Diagram

What is a Class? A class is a description of a group of objects with common properties (attributes like location, time), common behavior (operations), common relationships to other objects, and common semantics.

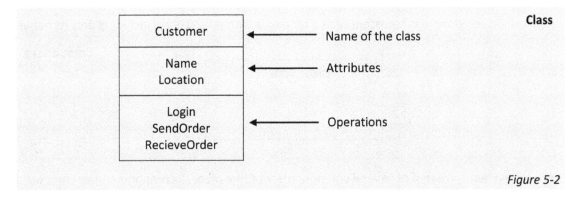

Figure 5-2

Class diagram describes the structure of a system by showing the system's classes, their attributes and the relationships among these classes. It explains the application graphically in a technical way where a common user cannot understand by looking at it.

It is a **static structure**: which means they display what interacts but not what happens when they interact.

Class diagrams are created by the <u>Architect</u> or the <u>Technical Lead (TL)</u>.

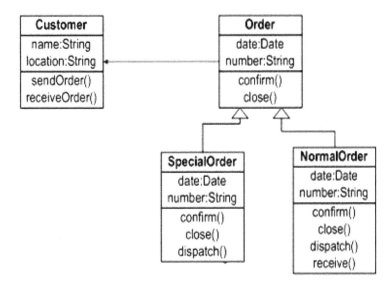

Figure 5-3

2. Component Diagram

What is a Component? A component is a physical and replaceable module of an application that conforms to and provides the realization of a set of interfaces. Components are composed of one or more classes or interfaces.

Graphically, a component is represented as a rectangle with tabs, usually including only its name.

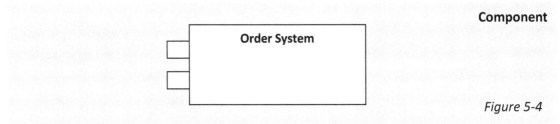

Component

Order System

Figure 5-4

Since the system is created of several components, not one piece, a component diagram is used to depict how the various components of a system and show the dependencies among these components.

Component Diagrams are used during the technical design and created by the <u>Architect</u> or the <u>Technical Lead (TL)</u>.

3. Deployment Diagram

Deployment diagrams show the physical relationship among software and hardware components in the system. They show how the component diagrams interact. In many cases developers combine the component and deployment diagrams into a single diagram.

Deployment diagrams are created by the <u>Architect</u> or the <u>Technical Lead (TL)</u>.

4. Package Diagram (Decomposition)

Package Diagrams are similar to Class Diagrams. However, instead of showing the individual classes, they show the related classes grouped together into a unit called a "Package". When the team deploys software it should always be packaged, related functionalities can be packaged together and then packaged with the overall application.

A dependency exists between two packages if any dependency exists between any two classes inside each package. Package Diagrams can be really useful to obtain an overview of a large system. Sometimes developers also choose to display the individual classes inside the packages.

Deployment diagrams are created by the <u>Architect</u> or the <u>Deployment Specialist</u>.

5. Statechart Diagram (State Machine Diagram)

What is a state? A state is a condition during the life of an object. It satisfies some condition, performs some action, or waits for an event.

The UML notation for a state is a rectangle with rounded corners as shown below in figure 5-5.

Figure 5-5

State diagram describes the behavior of a system where it shows all the possible states an object can get into. Mostly, State Diagrams are drawn to show the lifetime behavior of a single class. The large black dots indicate the starting and ending points of the events. State transition diagrams are drawn for objects that typically have a lot of dynamic behavior.

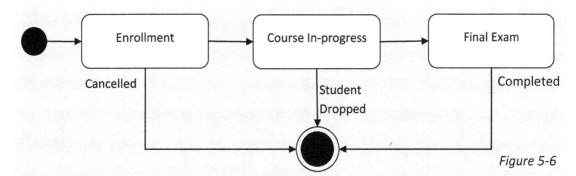

Figure 5-6

Statechart diagrams are created by the <u>Architect.</u>

6. Object Diagram

An object is an instance of a class. The object diagram is a static snapshot of a dynamic view that depicts a complete or partial view of the system at a specific time.

Object diagrams are created by the <u>Architect</u> or the <u>Developer</u>.

- Now you might ask, why should a BA know these diagrams if they are created by the Architects or Tech Leads? Well it's useful to be aware of all the diagrams used in the project, what are these diagrams used for and who is responsible for developing each diagram.
- By text books a BA is not supposed to create the <u>6</u> above mentioned diagrams, but in very rare situations you might be asked to create any of them. So no harm in knowing what they represent.
- As a BA you will be responsible for creating Sequence Diagrams, Activity Diagrams, Swim lane Diagrams and Use Cases.

- As a business analyst, what are the UML diagrams that you are responsible for? How do you create them?

7. Sequence Diagram

It is designed to show the users, stakeholders and technical team how the processing of messages will happen in a time oriented manner, where it displays the sequence of events between entities of the system to show the **dynamic view** of the system.

Sequence diagrams are executed line by line showing the time ordering of messages. Let's take a look at the following example:

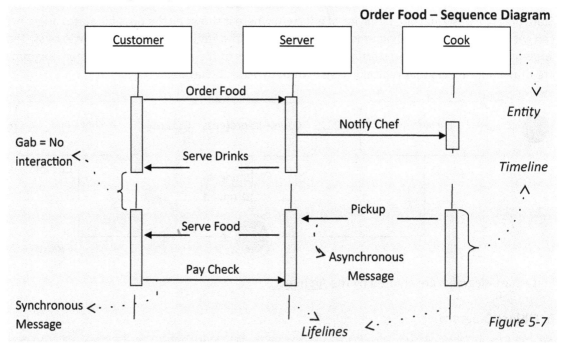

Figure 5-7

The diagram shows the different processes as vertical columns or lines, and the messages or interactions between them are represented by arrows with the arrowhead pointing towards the receiver – away from the sender. The name of the message is written above the message arrow line.

In this example, there are three entities – Customer, Server and Cook. The flow of messages can be read as follows:

1. The customer orders food from the server
2. Server will notify the cook to prepare the food and serve the drinks
3. Waiter will pick up the ready food from the cook and serve it to the customer
4. Customer will pay the check to the waiter

This is a simple example to show how the flow of messages can be represented using the sequence diagrams. Wherever there is gab in the timeline, it shows that there was no real interaction in that time period from the concerned entity.

The message sent between two entities can be synchronous or asynchronous:

- **Synchronous** message indicates that the sender will wait until the receiver has finished processing the message and only then proceed (represented by a solid-line arrow)
  - o In figure 5.6, "place order" is synchronous message because the customer (sender) orders food and waits for the server's (receiver) confirmation.

- **Asynchronous** message indicates that the sender will not wait for a response that the receiver has received and finished processing the message (represented by a hashed-line arrow)
  - o In figure 5.6, "serve food" is asynchronous message because the server (sender) does not need to wait for the customer (receiver) to respond. Server will just serve the food or drinks and leave.

8. Activity Diagram

Activity diagrams are similar to flow charts. They describe the sequencing of activities, actions, choices and system's logic. Like Statechart diagrams, the starting point is indicated with a large black dot. The horizontal black lines indicate where the object may take one of several different paths of action. Activity Diagrams are especially useful for objects which contain a lot of complex logic that you wish to clearly present.

Activity diagrams are typically used for business process modeling. They tell the story of the business process in a diagrammatic representation.

Symbols used in activity diagrams:

Symbol	Description
●	**Initial node:** it begins the workflow
↓	**Control flow:** Solid line arrow used to indicate direction of workflow (connects activity to activity)
⇣	**Object flow:** Represented by a dashed arrow (connects activity to object)
Activity	**An activity:** it is a task performed within the overall process
ObjectName:ClassName	**Object:** it is required, created or updated by an activity
Input → ◇ → Output A, Output B	**Decision:** a diamond represents a decision with alternate paths (Output A or B, cannot be both A and B) For example, it could be order accepted or rejected There is no restriction on the number of control flows exiting, a decision can have a three outgoing edges A predefined **guard** may be used. Guard is explained next
Input → ◇ → [Guard] = [Priority 1], [Priority=2], [else]	

[Guard] →	**Guard:** Represented in square brackets. A condition that may be added to a control flow. If the guard is true, the process flows along the control flow
Event →	**Event:** represented on a control flow to indicate a trigger. When the event occurs, it interrupts the preceding activity
Fork / Join (synchronization bar diagram)	**A synchronization** bar helps illustrate parallel transitions. Synchronization is also called Fork and Join
Fork Node diagram	**Fork Node:** it has one input and multiple outputs and is used to split incoming flow into multiple concurrent flows
Join Node diagram	**Join Node:** it has multiple inputs and one output and is used to synchronize incoming concurrent flows
Activity 1 → A, A → Activity 2	**Connector Node** is used to break up the diagram if it is too large (also called on-page connector). The connector node is usually used to break the diagram into more than one page. The diagram below represents the flow before adding the connector: Activity 1 → Activity 2
⊗	**Flow Final Node:** it terminates the flow
⊙	**Activity Final Node:** represents the final action state or the end of the process

Let's try using these symbols in the example below:

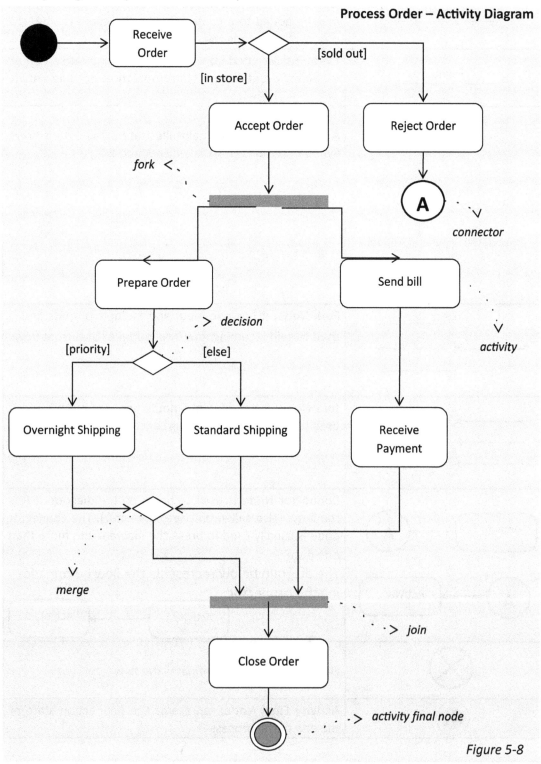

Figure 5-8

Reject Order – Activity Diagram

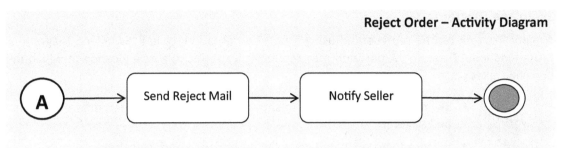

Figure 5-9

In this example, after an order is received a decision needs to be made by the sales department. If the product ordered is not available in store or sold out, the sales specialist rejects the order (a connector is used to avoid the diagram complexity, see figure 5-9), sends a reject mail to the customer and notifies the seller.

If the product ordered is available in store, the specialist accepts the order. Then he/she prepares the order for shipping and sends the bill to the customer (both actions are done concurrently). Note, that this process flow permits the order shipment regardless if the invoice is sent or payment is confirmed or not.

After the order is shipped (according to its priority) and payment is received, the order is closed and the activity ends.

- This diagram focuses on the flow of events or activities and their triggers regardless who is performing each activity.

- In activity diagrams, you can use a partition called a "Swimlane" to focus on representing actors performing activities. (Swimlane Diagram discussed next)

Swimlane Diagram

Activity Diagram can be represented using a partition notation, called "Swimlane Diagram or Cross-functional Diagram". A partition may represent a specific role or a location at which the behavior takes place.

- Swimlane diagram is used to show the interaction between different actors and systems.
- It keeps focus on high-level activities and who performs them
- It is ideal for working with stakeholders because it is very simple and easy to understand

The Swimlane notation is shown with two parallel lines, either horizontal or vertical, and a name labeling the partition in a box at one end. (See figures 5-10 and 5-11)

Horizontal Swimlane

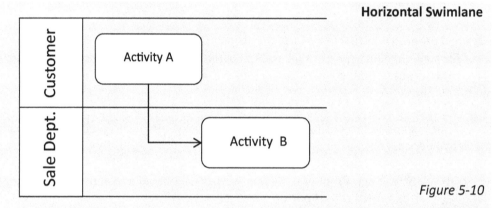

Figure 5-10

Now, let's see the same "Order Processing" example represented in a Swimlane Diagram:

Vertical Swimlane

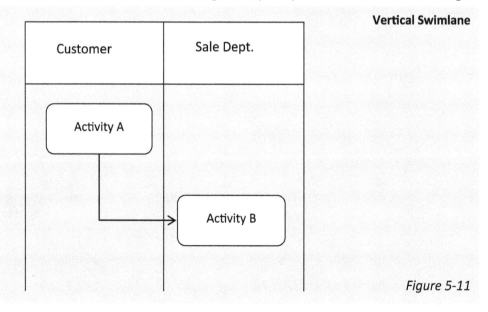

Figure 5-11

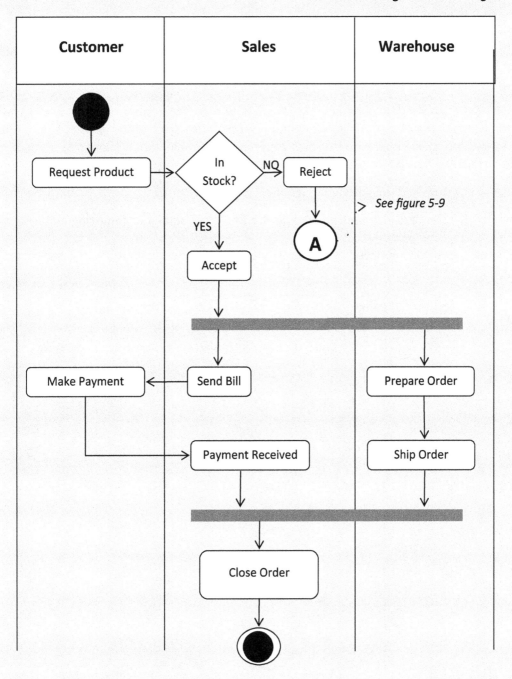

Order Processing – Swimlane Diagram

Figure 5-12

9. Use Case Diagram

Use case diagram represents a graphical overview of the functionality provided by the system in terms of actors, their goals (represented as use cases) and dependencies between them. The main purpose of the use case diagram is to show "**how does the functionality work?**" by illustrating the interaction between end user and the system from the user's perspective.

Use case diagrams are usually referred to as **behavior diagrams** because they are used to depict the behavior of the system and show "**how does the system respond to the end user interactions**"? They are a brilliant way of representing the nature of the existing/future function in a very simple pictorial way so that even a common stakeholder (non-technical) can understand the system and how it responds to the user interaction.

 Quick TIP

- Use case diagrams define the system from the user's perspective
- It is also used to analyze the impact of adding or removing features to the system

Let's see how the "Order Food" example (figure 5-7) can be represented by a use case:

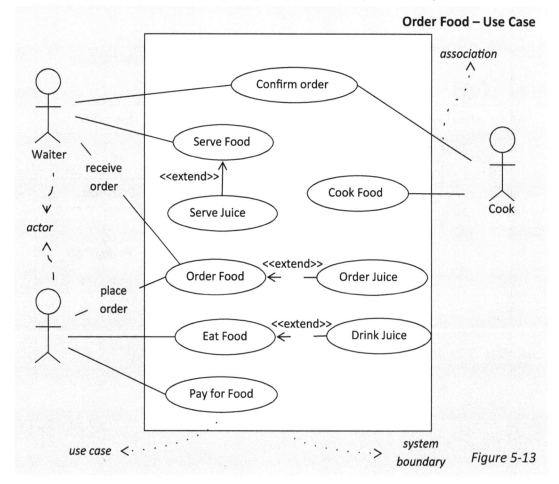

Order Food – Use Case

Figure 5-13

- What are the components of a use case?
- Walk me through a use case.
- How do you write a use case?

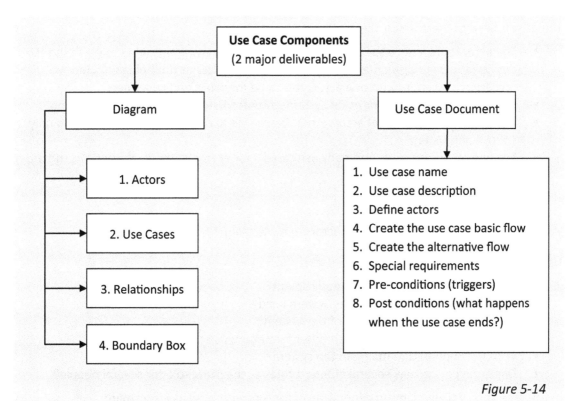

Use Case Components
(2 major deliverables)

Diagram

1. Actors

2. Use Cases

3. Relationships

4. Boundary Box

Use Case Document

1. Use case name
2. Use case description
3. Define actors
4. Create the use case basic flow
5. Create the alternative flow
6. Special requirements
7. Pre-conditions (triggers)
8. Post conditions (what happens when the use case ends?)

Figure 5-14

How do you write a use case?

1. Define your actors
2. Define their goals
3. Define the system's use cases (you can uses the actors goals as high level use cases)
4. Identify the relationship between:
   i.   Actors and actors
   ii. Use cases and use cases
   iii. Actors and uses cases
5. Create the use case document

1. Actors

Actors are not part of the system; they represent any person or system that interacts with the application. An actor represents a specific role that we do not have control of, the actor will do something to the use case and the use case will respond to the actor's action.

Things you need to know about the actor:

- The actor represents a specific role – not all people playing the same role – in the "Order Food" example, we may have more than one waiter or multiple cooks but we still represent all waiters with one actor, and same for cooks and customers
- Actors can be end users or other systems interacting with the function represented
- We do not have control of actors – actors are free to do what they want, we can only control our system
- A single actor may carry out many use cases – for example, the cook confirms the order and cooks food

    ▪ How do you identify actors in a use case?

Use the following questions to identify actors:

- Who is interested in a certain requirement?
- Where in the organization is the system used?
- Who will benefit from the use of the system?
- Who will supply the system with this information; use this information?
- Who will support and maintain the system?
- Does one person play several different roles or the same role for several people?

In use case and UML diagrams in general, an actor is represented as a stickman:

Figure 5-15

Now that you have identified your actors, the following logical step is to define the goals of each actor:

- Waiter goals are to take order from customer, confirm order with the cook and serve food to customer
- Customer goals are to order food, eat food and pay for his/her order
- Cook goals are to confirm the order with the waiter and cook food

Once you have identified your actors and their goals, you have now created your initial list of high level use cases. Remember, effective use cases must have understandable actors and goals.

2. Use Cases

Within the use case diagram there are several use cases. A use case represents a certain functionality or capability provided to the actors by the system. A group of use cases (functions) for a system define the ways the system can be used.

In UML diagrams, a use case is represented as an ellipse. The use case name can be placed either inside (figure 5-16) or below it (figure 5-17):

Figure 5-16   **Confirm Oder**   *Figure 5-17*

- A use case typically represents a complete functionality that the actor can use in a system.
- A use case must deliver something of value to an actor.

- How do you identify the use cases for a system?

Use the following questions to identify use cases:
- What are the goals of each actor?
- How can each actor achieve their goal?
- Will any actor create, store, modify, delete, or read information in the system?
- Does any actor need to be notified about certain occurrences in the system?
- What are the functions currently in the system or need to be created?

In the food order example the use cases are:
- Confirm order
- Serve food
- Seeve drinks
- Cook food
- Eat food
- Drink
- Pay check

3. Use Case Relationships (Associations)

An association relationship indicates the communication between an actor and a use case. A communication association can flow in both directions (actor to use case and use case to actor) and it is represented with a solid line connecting the two parties and in some cases with an arrowhead. The arrowhead represents who is initiating the use case.

The following are the use case relationships:

- **Generalization Relationship**

Generalization relationship is defined by UML 2.0 as, "A taxonomic relationship between a more general classifier and a more specific classifier. Each instance of the specific classifier is also an indirect instance of the general classifier. Thus the specific classifier indirectly has features of the more general classifier."

In the food order example, when an object belongs to a specialized class (for example, cook steak and cook pasta), this automatically implies that it belongs to a generalization of that class (for example, cook food.) Furthermore, any attribute or operation that applies to the generalized class also applies to the specialized class.

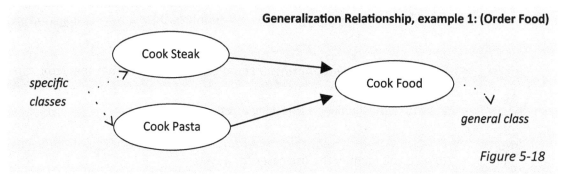

Generalization Relationship, example 1: (Order Food)

Figure 5-18

One more example:

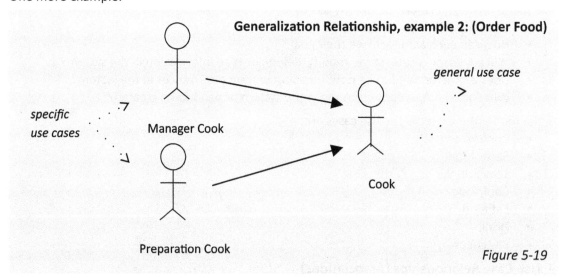

Generalization Relationship, example 2: (Order Food)

Figure 5-19

- In a generalization relationship, think of the general use case as a "parent" use case
- Specific use cases inherit the behavior of the general use case

- Include Relationship

Include relationships describe a <u>required</u> (non-optional) behavior included in the base use case. Sometimes this is called a "uses relationship" because it is a relationship created between a use case (base) that "uses" the functionality of another use case (included). Generally, it is assumed that the included use case will be called every time the basic path is run.

For example, pay for food use case includes swiping credit card and the customer needs to sign the check use cases. Note that the included use cases are required for the base use case and not optional.

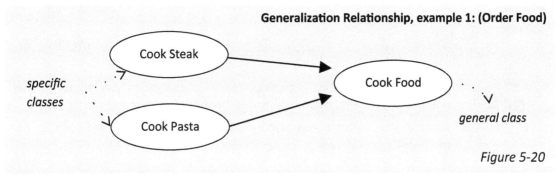

Figure 5-20

Include relationship could also be as follow:

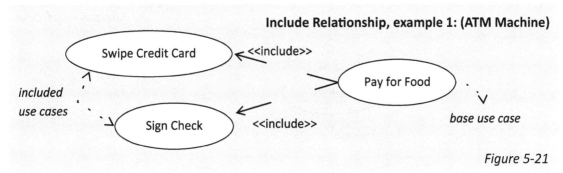

Figure 5-21

In this example, both Deposit and Withdraw use cases require (include) Insert PIN use case.

- An include relationship is represented as a dependency relationship that points from the base use case to the used (included) use case
- The base use case "uses" the included uses case
- A base use case cannot function till it gets information from the included use case

- Extend Relationship

In this relationship, an extension use case is created to extend the behavior of the extended (base) use case when exceptional circumstances are encountered. An extend relationship is used to represent an <u>optional</u> or <u>exceptional</u> behavior.

For example in figure 5-22, the "order juice" use case is an extend relationship because it is not a mandatory aspect (optional), the customer may or may not order juice and it extends the behavior of the order food use case.

Extend Relationship, example: (Order Food)

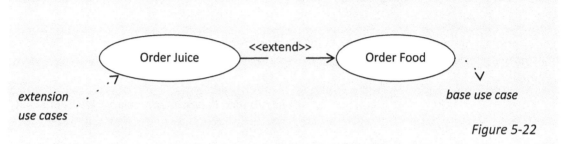

extension
use cases

base use case

Figure 5-22

- An extend relationship is represented as a dependency relationship that points from the extension use case to the base use case
- An extension use case may also include an extension use case itself (see figure 5-23)

The difference between include and extend relationships might get confusing, so let's see a very simple example with both relationships:

Amazon – Use Case

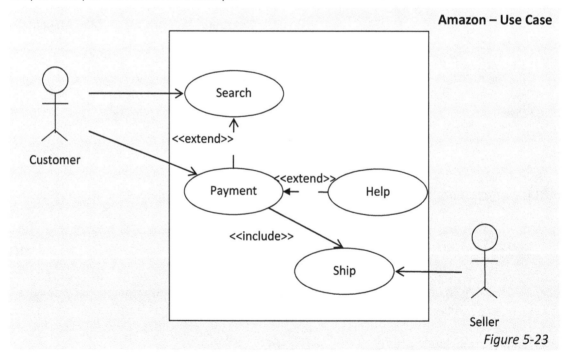

Figure 5-23

An extend relationship between the "search" and "payment" use cases, because the "payment" use case is extending the "search" use case, therefore it is an <u>exceptional</u> behavior where customers will only make the payment if they find the item they are looking for. Note that the "payment" use case itself has an extend relationship with "help" use case.

On the other hand, the relationship between the "ship" and "payment" use cases is an include relationship because it is mandatory to make the shipment once the payment is done, therefore it is a <u>required</u> behavior to the base use case.

Generalization vs. Include vs. Extend relationships

Generalization	Include	Extend
Food ◄— Steak	Deposit cash → Insert PIN <<include>>	Login ◄— Help <<extend>>
Specialized use case is required	Included uses case is required	Extension use case is optional
The arrow points from the specialized use case to the general (base) use case	The arrow points from the base use case to the used (included) use case	The arrow points from the extension use case to the base use case
Used when you have an "is-a-kind-of" relationship	Used when you have use case that is dependent on another use case or needs information from the other use case to function	Used when you have an optional behavior that you need to add
Base use case can be complete or incomplete by itself	Base use case is incomplete by itself, it needs the included use case to function completely	Base use case is complete by itself, it can function independently

- When should you use generalization, include and exclude relationships?

4. System Boundary

The system boundary box is a rectangular shape drawn around the concerned use case to represent the system's scope. Only the use cases contained within that boundary box are considered to be in-scope, other than that is considered out-of-scope.

Use Case Document

The use case could be included in the Business Requirement Document (BRD) or a separate document depending on the organization you are working for. The components of a use case document are:

1. Use case name: assign a unique name to your use case preferably describing the functionality you want to present (like food order, order processing or ATM machine)

2. Brief description of the use case – the description can be in any of the following formats:

   a. Narrative: it is describing the user's intent from the use case in a free form text; it tells the story of the user's actions during the use case

   b. Scenario: it is describing the sequence of events and the list of steps to accomplish; it is a simple step by step statement in logical sequence, such as in ATM machine:

      i. Present transaction screen

      ii. Capture fast cash withdrawal request

      iii. Post transaction to bank and confirm

      iv. Dispense money, card and transaction receipt

   c. Conversation: it is describing the use case behavior in a dialogue form between the user and the system, such as:

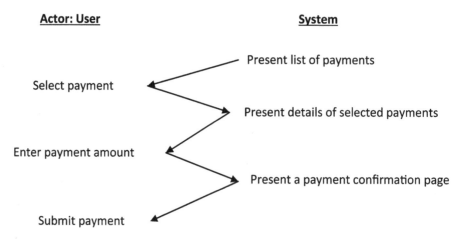

Actor: User	System
	Present list of payments
Select payment	
	Present details of selected payments
Enter payment amount	
	Present a payment confirmation page
Submit payment	

- You can use any of the above formats to describe your use case as long as it's clear and easy for the stakeholders to understand

3. Define actors: in this section you will basically list all your actors, their role description and their objectives.

Actor/Role Name	Role Description and Objective
Actor	Briefly describe the role of the actor to the system and how the actor will use the system What is the actor's goal? What does the actor need from the system? What is the expected outcome from the system?
Customer	Customer will place food order and may or may not order juice. When the order is served, customer will eat his/her meal and pay the check
Waiter	Waiter will receive the food order from customer and confirm order with the cook and serve food to customer

4. Create the <u>basic flow:</u> the basic flow represents the most important course of events or what happens most of the time, sometimes called a "happy day scenario" because it occurs when everything goes well (no errors). The benefits of creating the basic flow is that it once the norm is understood – which represents 70% of the system – it is easier to comprehend exceptions

5. Create the alternative flow – the alternative flow could be a variation or exception:

    a. Variation: it is also referred to as an additional flow, which is another significant way to accomplish the same function that could be taken at this point (not necessarily error based). For example you can press (CTRL + S) to save a document or click on menu then click save. Another example, you can enter your username and password then hit ENTER or click on the LOGIN button

    b. Exception: it describes anything that could go wrong (error), like what would happen if the user enters a wrong password? The system sends an error message

6. Special requirements: it describes any limitations to the function. For example, wire transfer limit is $500 or country limitations for international calls

7. Pre-conditions: it represents the preconditions that must be met before this use case can start. In other words, what triggers the function to start? For example, the user needs to sign-in to be able to send an email

8. Post conditions: what should happen when the use case ends?

(See use case template in chapter 8)

- Not all use case documents include the entire list mentioned above; it depends on the level of detail you wish to achieve; however, providing more detail to stakeholders is beneficial
- We write it to a level that is appropriate to readers

Tools to create UML Diagrams

There are several tools that can be used to develop UML diagrams. Depending on the organization you are working for, they may use any of the following tools:

- Rational Rose: it comes with the Rational Suite (created by IBM). Rational Rose is the most respected in the business, but it is only used for huge projects because its license is very expensive
- Ms Visio: it is the most common used by many organizations (Microsoft Product)
- Visual Paradigm: it is very similar to Ms Visio for Macintosh users
- Enterprise Architect

UML Diagrams

WHAT?

o It is a modeling language which puts together several diagrammatic views that can be used at any stage of the software development life cycle to specify, visualize, modify, construct and document the system artifacts.

WHY?

o Developing a model for a software system prior to its development allows the team to design and plan the system they are building before wasting any time coding the wrong design

o Modeling is a very effective way for communication with stakeholders (customers, domain experts, designers, developers, etc.) and understanding the problem.

HOW?

There are several tools that can be used to develop UML diagrams. Depending on the organization you are working for, they may use any of the following tools:

o Rational Rose: it comes with the Rational Suite (created by IBM). Rational Rose is the most respected in the business, but it is only used for huge projects because its license is very expensive

o Ms Visio: it is the most common used by many organizations (Microsoft Product)

o Visual Paradigm: it is very similar to Ms Visio for Macintosh users

o Enterprise Architect

Diagram	Description	Responsibility
1. Class Diagram	Class diagram is a *static* representation of a solution. It shows the system's classes, their attributes and the relationships among these classes. It explains the application graphically in a technical way where a common user cannot understand by looking at it.	Created by the Architect or the Technical Lead (TL).
2. Component Diagram	A component is a physical and replaceable module of an application that conforms to and provides the realization of a set of interfaces. Components are composed of one or more classes or interfaces.	Created by the Architect or the Technical Lead (TL).
3. Deployment Diagram	Deployment diagrams show the physical relationship among software and hardware components in the system. They show how the component diagrams interact. In many cases developers combine the component and deployment diagrams into a single diagram.	Created by the Architect or the Technical Lead (TL).
4. Package Diagram (Decomposition)	Package Diagrams are similar to Class Diagrams. However, instead of showing the individual classes, they show the related classes grouped together into a unit called a "Package". When the team deploys software it should always look like a "Package", related functionalities can be packaged together and then packaged with the overall application.	Created by the Architect or the Deployment Specialist
5. Statechart Diagram (State Machine)	State diagram describes the behavior of a system where it shows all the possible states an object can get into. Mostly, State Diagrams are drawn to show the lifetime behavior of a single class.	Created by the Architect
6. Object Diagram	An object is an instance of a class. The object diagram is a static snapshot of a dynamic view that depicts a complete or partial view of the system at a specific time.	Created by the Architect or the Developer
7. Sequence Diagram	It is designed to show the users, stakeholders and technical team how the processing of messages will happen in a time oriented manner, where it displays the sequence of events between entities of the system to show the **dynamic view** of the system. Sequence diagrams are executed line by line showing the time ordering of messages	Created by the Business Analyst
8. Activity Diagram	Activity diagram is similar to flow chart. It describes the sequencing of activities, actions, choices and system's logic. Activity diagram is typically used for business process modeling. It tells the story of the business process in a diagrammatic representation.	Created by the Business Analyst
9. Use Case Diagram	Use case diagram represents a graphical overview of the functionality provided by the system in terms of actors, their goals (represented as use cases) and dependencies between them. The main purpose of the use case diagram is to show **"how does the functionality work?"** by illustrating the interaction between end user and the system from the user's perspective. They are a brilliant way of representing the nature of the existing/future function in a very simple pictorial way so that even a common stakeholder (non-technical) can understand the system and how it responds to the user interaction.	Created by the Business Analyst

Introduction to SQL

Structured Query Language (SQL)

As a business analyst you may get exposed to some SQL related tasks and projects, so this chapter is designed to introduce you to the basic SQL queries and statements. You will learn how to execute basic queries against a database to perform different activities such as retrieve, insert, delete or update data from tables located in a database.

- A 3D business analyst is the one who is knowledgeable of all tasks in his/her project.
- Learn to speak to your team members each with their own language.

What is SQL?

SQL is an acronym for Structured Query Language. It is a computer programming language used to manage and retrieve data in relational database management system (RDBMS), create and modify the database schema.

In brief, let's summarize what can be done with SQL:
1. Query the database – it allows you to query data held in the database and have a result set returned, which could be a simple one line or several pages of text
2. Data Manipulation Language (DML) – statements or commands used to modify data held within a database, such as removing data or inserting new data
3. Data Definition Language (DDL) – commands used to change the database schema (structure) by creating new database objects like tables, indexes, etc
4. Querying more than one table in a database

SQL Database Tables
A database most often contains one or more tables. Each table is identified by a name (e.g. "Clients", "Employees" or "Purchases") and contains records with data.

Database Table Components:
1. Table name
2. Columns
3. Rows
4. Fields

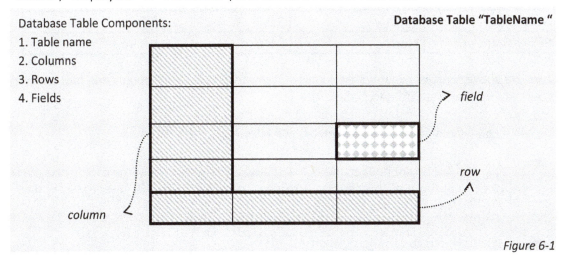

Figure 6-1

Table Properties

- The table name should be unique
- Each row is unique
- A row is identified by a primary key (will be explained later in this chapter)
- There cannot be any duplication in column names
- Row and column order are not important, the row's default order is the order in which they were inserted into a table

Below is an example of two tables in a database – we shall be using these tables throughout the chapter:

Table 1 called "Students":

LastName	FirstName	Gender	Address
Thompson	Mark	Male	122 Street
Erik	Tom	Male	15 Street
Walsh	Penny	Female	24 Street
Ibrahim	Nadia	Female	100 Street

The table above contains four rows, each row contains records for each student, and four columns (LastName, FirstName, Gender, Address).

Table 2 called "Courses"

CourseName	StartDate	Tuition	Location
Marketing	June	$250	Paris
Human Resources	April	$600	London
Finance	October	$500	New York
Accounting	January	$550	Cairo
Business Analysis	March	$450	Cairo

The table above contains five rows, each row contains records for each course and four columns (CourseName, StartDate, Tuition, Location).

You can <u>query</u> a database via SQL statements and have a <u>result set</u> returned.

- You do not need to memorize the syntax or worry about the coding part. The purpose of this chapter is to understand the basic SQL queries, what they mean and how they work.

1. Retrieve Data

- **The SELECT Statement**

It is a command used to select data from a table located in a database.

Syntax: SELECT "column_name" FROM "table_name";

Query: SELECT CourseName FROM Course;

Result:

CourseName

Marketing
Human Resources
Finance
Accounting
Business Analysis

To select more than one column: SELECT CourseName, StartDate FROM Course

Result:

CourseName	StartDate
Marketing	June
Human resources	April
Finance	October
Accounting	January
Business Analysis	March

To select all columns from the Courses table, use a (*) symbol instead of column names, like this:

SELECT * FROM Courses;

Result:

CourseName	StartDate	Tuition	Location
Marketing	June	$250	Paris
Human resources	April	$600	London
Finance	October	$500	New York
Accounting	January	$550	Cairo
Business Analysis	March	$450	Cairo

- **The SELECT DISTINCT Statement**

The SELECT statement allows you to retrieve all records from a column(s) on a table; this means that there will be redundancies (i.e., Cairo in the "Courses" table is mentioned twice in the "Location" column). What if you want to prevent duplicate rows from being selected? All you need to do is to add a DISTINCT keyword to the SELECT statement:

Syntax: SELECT DISTINCT "column_name(s)" FROM "table_name";
Query: SELECT DISTINCT Location FROM Courses;

Result:

Location

Paris

London

New York

Cairo

The ORDER BY Clause

The order of data selected is undefined. You can sort the selected data by using the ORDER BY clause.

Syntax: SELECT "column_name" FROM "table_name" ORDER BY "column_name";
Query: SELECT CourseName, Tuition, Location FROM Courses ORDER BY Tuition;
Result:

CourseName	Tuition	Location
Marketing	$250	Paris
Business Analysis	$450	Cairo
Finance	$500	New York
Accounting	$550	Cairo
Human Resources	$600	London

Note that the default sorting is by an ascending order. If you want to change the sorting into descending order, use DESC after the column_name.

- **The WHERE Clause**

Now, you might need to conditionally select data from a table. For example, you may want to only retrieve courses with tuition above $550. To do that, use the WHERE clause:

Syntax: SELECT "column_name" FROM "table_name" WHERE "operator value";
These are the operator values you can use:

Operator	Description
=	Equal
<	Less than
<=	Less than or equal to
>	Greater than
>=	Greater than or equal to

<>	Not equal to
BETWEEN-AND	Select a range between two values
LIKE	Search for pattern

Query: SELECT CourseName FROM Courses WHERE Tuition > 550;
Result:

CourseName

Human Resources

The IN Operator

The IN operator is used if you know the exact value you want to return for at least one of the columns.

Syntax:

SELECT "column_name"
FROM "table_name"
WHERE "column_name" IN ('value1', 'value2', ...);

Query:

SELECT *
FROM Courses
WHERE CourseName IN (Finance, Accounting, Business Analysis);
Result:

CourseName	**StartDate**	**Tuition**	**Location**
Finance	October	$500	New York
Accounting	January	$550	Cairo
Business Analysis	March	$450	Cairo

The BETWEEN-AND Operator

Whereas the IN operator allows you to limit the selection criteria to one or more discrete values, the BETWEEN operator allows you to select a range between two values.
Syntax:

SELECT "column_name"
FROM "table_name"
WHERE "column_name" BETWEEN 'value1' AND 'value';

Query:

SELECT *
FROM Courses

WHERE Tuition BETWEEN '199' AND '499';

Result:

CourseName	StartDate	Tuition	Location
Marketing	June	$250	Paris
Business Analysis	March	$450	Cairo

The LIKE Operator

LIKE is another keyword that can be used in the WHERE clause. Basically, LIKE allows you to do a search on a pattern rather than specifying exactly what is desired (as in IN) or spell out a range (as in BETWEEN).

Syntax:

SELECT "column_name"
FROM "table_name"
WHERE "column_name" LIKE 'pattern';
Pattern consists of wildcards, such as:

Wildcard	Description
A_X	All strings that start with (A)+ only one character + end with (Z). For example, (AdX) and (A9X) would both satisfy the condition, while (ADF4X) would not because there is more than one character between the (A) and (X)
%A	All strings that end with (A). For example, if you use pattern (%G) in Course-Name column from the Courses table, the result will be (Marketing, Accounting)
A%	All strings that start with (A). For example, if you use pattern (J%) in StartDate column from the Courses table, the result will be (January, June)
%AN%	All strings that contain the pattern (AN) anywhere. Like Human Resources, Finance, Accounting in the courses table

Query:

SELECT *
FROM Courses
WHERE CourseName LIKE '%AN%';

Result:

CourseName	StartDate	Tuition	Location
Human resources	April	$600	London
Finance	October	$500	New York
Business Analysis	March	$450	Cairo

The AND-OR Operator

The WHERE keyword can be a simple condition (as presented in the previous examples), or it can be compound condition. Compound conditions are made up of multiple simple conditions connected by AND or OR.

- AND & OR joins two or more conditions in a WHERE clause
- AND returns a row if <u>ALL</u> conditions listed are true
- OR returns a row if <u>ANY</u> of the conditions listed are true

<u>Syntax:</u>

SELECT "column_name"
FROM "table_name"
WHERE "column_name"
AND/OR 'simple condition';

<u>OR Query:</u>

SELECT *
FROM Courses
WHERE Tuition < 499
OR = '600';
<u>OR Result:</u>

CourseName	StartDate	Tuition	Location
Marketing	June	$250	Paris
Human resources	April	$600	London
Business Analysis	March	$450	Cairo

Note the difference between the results for the OR and AND queries. OR keyword returned the Marketing and Business Analysis courses because their tuition is less than $499 and also returned the Human Resources course because its tuition = $600 (<u>any</u> condition is satisfied). In the example below, let's replace OR keyword with AND:

<u>AND Query:</u>

SELECT *
FROM Courses
WHERE Tuition < 499
AND = '600';

<u>AND Result:</u>

NULL

It returned NULL (nothing or no value) because <u>all</u> conditions (less than $499 and =$600) have to be satisfied, which is not true.

2. SQL Data Manipulation Language (DML)

So far, all of the SQL statements we have looked at have had to do with querying data, using the SELECT statement. Now we are ready to take a look at other types of SQL commands: DML. DML is used to modify data held within the database using syntax like:

- INSERT INTO – to insert new data into a database table
- UPDATE – to update data in a database table
- DELETE – to delete data from a database table

- **The INSERT INTO Statement**

You can use the INSERT INTO command if you need to create new data within the database. This allows you to create/insert new rows into any table (as long as you have the correct privileges).

Syntax:

INSERT INTO "table_name" (column1, column2, ...)
VALUES (value1, value2, ...) ;

Query:

INSERT INTO Students (LastName, FirstName, Gender, Address)
VALUES (Vieira, Erica, Female, 88 Street);

The above query says: insert a new row into the students table, set the LastName column to Vieira, FirstName to Erica, Gender to Female and Address to 88 Street.

Result:

LastName	FirstName	Gender	Address
Thompson	Mark	Male	122 Street
Erik	Tom	Male	15 Street
Walsh	Penny	Female	24 Street
Ibrahim	Nadia	Female	100 Street
Vieira	Erica	Female	88 Street

The INSERT INTO statement can be used in various ways:

- Insert a row in Students table only specifying required columns (LastName and First-Name), such as:

INSERT INTO Students (LastName, FirstName)
VALUES (Vieira, Erica);

LastName	FirstName	Gender	Address
Vieira	Erica	-	-

Insert a row in students table using the courses table
INSERT INTO Students (LastName)

(SELECT CourseName FROM Courses);

- **The UPDATE Statement**

The UPDATE statement is used if you want to modify or update some data within a database table.

Syntax:

UPDATE "table_name"

SET "column_name" = "new_value"

WHERE "condition";

Query:

UPDATE Students

SET Tuition = $1000

WHERE Location = Cairo;

The above query says: find all courses located in Cairo and update their tuition to $1000.

Result:

CourseName	StartDate	Tuition	Location
Marketing	June	$250	Paris
Human resources	April	$600	London
Finance	October	$500	New York
Accounting	January	$1000	Cairo
Business Analysis	March	$1000	Cairo

- **The DELETE Statement**

The DELETE statement is used to remove a single or multiple rows in a database table.

Syntax:

DELETE FROM "table_name"

WHERE (condition);

Query:

DELETE FROM Courses

WHERE CourseName = Finanace;

Result:

CourseName	StartDate	Tuition	Location
Marketing	June	$250	Paris

Human resources	April	$600	London
Accounting	January	$1000	Cairo
Business Analysis	March	$1000	Cairo

You can use (*) to DELETE all rows from a table, such as:

DELETE * FROM Courses

This will delete all rows in the Courses table but will not delete the table. The table will remain empty in the database.

- **TRUNCATE TABLE**

This is another effective way to delete data from a table. It is a very fast way to clear out tables with many hundreds of thousands or millions rows.

Syntax:

TRUNCATE TABLE "table_name";

Query:

TRUNCATE TABLE Courses

Note that in DELETE and TRUNCATE statements, you only remove data held in the table but you do not delete the entire table from the database. The table remains empty in the database. In the next section, we will cover the SQL DDL statements used to remove the table from a database.

3. SQL Data Definition Language (DDL)

Data Definition Language (DDL) is used to modify the database structure or schema. It is the part of SQL that allows you to create or delete tables. The most famous DDL statements in SQL are:

- CREATE TABLE – creates a new database table
- ALTER TABLE – changes a database table
- DROP TABLE – deletes a database table

- **The CREATE TABLE Statement**

The CREATE TABLE command is used to create new tables within the database.

Syntax:

CREATE TABLE "table_name"
(column_name type (size)
,column_name type (size), ...);

```
Some common SQL data types

Numeric            Character          Date
NUMBER             CHAR               DATE
INTEGER            VARCHAR
SMALLINT
DECIMAL
```

Query:

CREATE TABLE Members

(MemberID Number

, Name   VARCHAR2(12)

, Address   VARCHAR2(12));

The above query says: create a table named Members; the table consists of three columns: a numbers column called Member ID, a 12 digit VARCHAR2 column called Name and another 12 digit VARCHAR2 column called Address.

Result:

MemberID	Name	Address

- **The ALTER TABLE statement**

This command allows you to modify or make changes in the table structure, like adding an extra column to a table:

Syntax:

ALTER TABLE "table_name"

ADD (column_name type(size));

Query:

ALTER TABLE Members

ADD (Age Number);

This query will add a column called Age to the table Members.

Result:

MemberID	Name	Address	Age

- **The DROP TABLE Statement**

To entirely remove a table from the database you can use the DROP TABLE command.

Query:

DROP TABLE Members;

Note that once a table is removed, all data in this table is removed and cannot be recovered.

SQL DDL can also be used for:

- CREATE INDEX – creates an index (search key)
- DROP INDEX – deletes an index
- CREATE SYNONYM
- GRANT/REVOKE
- CREATE VIEW
- DROP VIEW
- CREATE SEQUENCE
- DROP SEQUENCE
- And others…

4. Querying More Than One Table

I. JOINS

In some cases you would need to select data from two or more tables to create a complete result. JOINS operation is used to query more than one table at the same time by relating tables in a database to each other with primary keys.

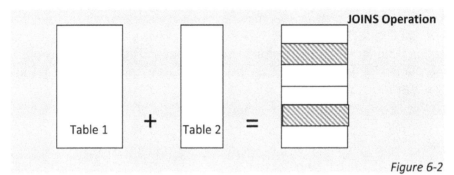

Figure 6-2

What is a primary key?

A primary key is a column within a database that has a unique value for each row. Let's have a look at the example below:

Table **Sales_Agent:**

AgentID	Name	Sales	Position
01	Thompson, Mark	$2000	Senior
02	Andre, Tony	$6500	Area Manager
03	Enright, Heidi	$4000	Junior
04	Andre, Tony	$3200	Junior

Table **Area:**

CityID	City	AgentID
201	New York	01
202	Alexandria	02
203	Moscow	03
204	Rome	04

In the "Sales_Agent" table above, the "AgentID" is the primary key, which means that no two rows can have the same Agent ID. The agent ID distinguishes between the sales agents even if they have the same name (like in agent 02 and 04, they have the same name but they are two different sales agents with different information).

Similarly in the "Area" table, the "CityID" is the primary key. The "AgentID" in the Area table is used to refer to the agents in the "Sales_Agent" table without actually using their names.

- The purpose of using keys is to bind data together, across tables, without repeating all of the data in every table.

Now let's go back to the JOINS operator:

To be able to do JOINS correctly in SQL, requires many of the elements we have introduced in this chapter so far (like SELECT and WHERE). For example, if you want to find out the sales by city. You can see that table "Area" includes information on cities and agents, and table "Sales_Agent" contains information for each agent and their sales amount in dollars. Note that the two tables are linked via "AgentID" common field.

Syntax:
SELECT "table1_name"."Column1name", "table2_name"."column2_name"
FROM "table1_name"."table2_name";
Query:
SELECT Sales_Agent.Sales, Area.City

FROM Sales_Agent, Area;

Result:

Sales	City
$2000	New York
$6500	Alexandria
$4000	Moscow
$3200	Rome

Let's see one more JOINS example: you want to find out which agent is accountable for which area.

Query:

SELECT Sales_Agent.Name, Area.City
FROM Sales_Agent, Area;

Result:

Name	City
Thompson, Mark	New York
Andre, Tony	Alexandria
Enright, Heidi	Moscow
Andre, Tony	Rome

II.   UNION

The purpose of the SQL UNION command is to combine the results of two queries together. That being said, UNION is somewhat similar to JOIN in that they both are used to relate information from multiple tables.

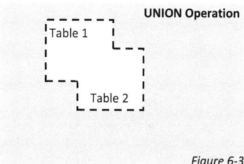

Figure 6-3

The UNION operator retrieves data that appear in either or both of two tables in a database. When using UNION, only distinct values are selected (similar to DISTINCT SELECT)

Syntax:

(SQL Statement 1)
UNION
(SQL Statement 2)
Let's see the following example:
Table **Employee**

Name	Sales	City
Thompson, Mark	$2000	London
Andre, Tony	$6500	Beijing
Enright, Heidi	$4000	Ontario
Kriner, Thom	$3200	Luxor

Table **Sales**

City	Sales
Paris	$10000
Rome	$5000
Berlin	$4550
Luxor	$15000

Let's say for example we want to find out all the cities where there are sales transactions. To do so, we use the UNION operator to select all the cities in both tables as follows:

Query:

SELECT City FROM Employee
UNION

SELECT City FROM Sales;
Result:

City

London

Beijing

Ontario

Luxor

Paris

Rome

Berlin

- Note that UNION operator only selects distinct values, so you only see Luxor once in the result set. Also, if we used "SELECT DISTINCT City" for either or both of the SQL statements, we will get the same result set.
- UNION acts as an <u>OR</u> operator (value is in table 1 OR table 2)

UNION ALL

The UNION ALL command also combines the results of two queries together like the UNION command. The difference between UNION ALL and UNION is that, while UNION only selects distinct values, UNION ALL selects all values.

So using the same example:

Syntax:

(SQL Statement 1)

UNION ALL

(SQL Statement 2)

Query:

SELECT City FROM Employee

UNION ALL

SELECT City FROM Sales;

Result:

City

London

Beijing

Ontario

Luxor

Paris

Rome

Berlin

Luxor

III. INTERSECT

Similar to the UNION command, INTERSECT also operates on two SQL statements. The difference is that, while UNION essentially acts as an OR operator, the INTERSECT command acts as an <u>AND</u> operator where value is selected only if it appears in table 1 and table 2.

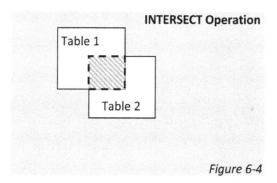

Figure 6-4

Syntax:

(SQL Statement 1)

INTERSECT

(SQL Statement 2)

The INTERSECT statement retrieves all records that appear in both tables. It combines the results of statement 1 and statement 2 and returns only data which appear in both queries.

Let's demonstrate with the following example using the tables Employee and Sales. If we want to find out all the cities that are in <u>both</u> tables:

 Query:

SELECT City FROM Employee

INTERSECT

SELECT City FROM Sales;

Result:

City

Luxor

- INTERESECT command only returns distinct value.

IV.   Minus

The MINUS operator combines the results of two or more tables and returns only data that appear in the first table after subtracting the second table. If the second table includes rows that are not present in the first table, such rows are ignored.

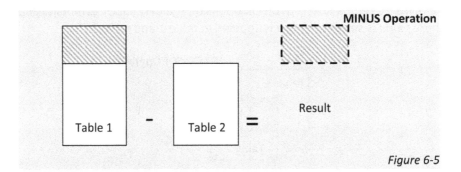

Figure 6-5

Syntax:

(SQL Statement 1)
MINUS
(SQL Statement 2)
Using the same Employee and Sales tables, if we want to find out what cities are in table 1 but not in table 2:

Query:

SELECT City FROM Employee
MINUS
SELECT City FROM Sales;
Result:

City

London

Beijing

Ontario

In the example above the MINUS equation = Employee table – Sales table, the cities London, Beijing and Ontario are in the employee table but not in the Sales table.

Now note the difference when we use Sales table – Employee table:

Query:

SELECT City FROM Sales

MINUS

SELECT City FROM Employee;

Result:

City

Paris

Rome

Berlin

5. Built-In Functions in SQL

SQL has many built-in functions; in this chapter we will just mention some of the counting and calculations functions to give you a chance to understand these functions and their description.

Aggregate Functions

Aggregate functions operate against multiple values and return a single value. Here are some of the most commonly used functions:

Function	Description
AVG (column)	Used to calculate the average value of a column
COUNT (column)	Used to calculate the number of rows in a column
COUNT (*)	Used to return the number of selected rows
FIRST (column)	It returns the value of the first row in a specific column
LAST (column)	It returns the value of the last row in a specific column
MAX (column)	Used to return the highest value in a column
MIN (column)	Used to return the lowest value in a column
SUM (column)	Used to calculate the sum of the values of records in a column

Syntax:

SELECT function (column) FROM table;

Let's assume we have the table **Sales** below and we want to calculate the average, maximum and total sales:

City	Amount
Paris	$1,000
Rome	$5,000
Berlin	$4,500
Luxor	$1,500
Las Vegas	$2,000
Boston	$1,000

Query:

SELECT AVG (Amount) FROM Sales;
SELECT MAX (Amount) FROM Sales;
SELECT SUM (Amount) FROM Sales;

Result:

AVG	$2,500
Max	$5,000
SUM	$15,000

Conclusion

Again, in most organizations you most probably will not be asked to create code, but you will be involved in discussions where you might hear something like, "We are using DDL to do something". So as a 3D Business Analyst you should know that they are talking about commands to change the table schema like creating new tables to the database you are talking about or, "Hey, would it work if we used JOINS function to do...", and so on!

What is SQL?

SQL is an acronym for Structured Query Language. It is a computer programming language used to manage and retrieve data in relational database management system (RDBMS), create and modify the database schema.

What can be done with SQL?

1. Query the database – it allows you to query data held in the database and have a result set returned, which could be a simple one line or several pages of text
2. Data Manipulation Language (DML) – statements or commands used to modify data held within a database, such as removing data or inserting new data
3. Data Definition Language (DDL) – commands used to change the database schema (structure) by creating new database objects like tables, indexes, etc
4. Querying more than one table in a database

SQL Database Tables

A database most often contains one or more tables. Each table is identified by a name (e.g. "Clients", "Employees" or "Purchases") and contains records with data.

Database Table Components:
1. Table name
2. Columns
3. Rows
4. Fields

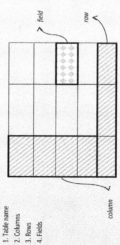

Table Properties

- The table name should be unique
- Each row is unique
- A row is identified by a primary key
- There cannot be any duplication in column names
- Row and column order are not important, the row's default order is the order in which they were inserted into a table

---

1. Retrieve Data

The SELECT Statement

It is a command used to select data from a table located in a database.

Syntax: SELECT "column_name" FROM "table_name";

The SELECT DISTINCT Statement

The SELECT statement allows you to retrieve all records from a column(s) on a table; this means that there will be redundancies. If you want to prevent duplicate rows from being selected, all you need to do is to add a DISTINCT keyword to the SELECT statement:

Syntax: SELECT DISTINCT "column_name(s)" FROM "table_name";

The ORDER BY Clause

The order of data selected is undefined. You can sort the selected data by using the ORDER BY clause.

Syntax: SELECT "column_name" FROM "table_name" ORDER BY "column_name";

The WHERE Clause

It is used to conditionally select data from a table.

Syntax: SELECT "column_name" FROM "table_name" WHERE "operator value";

These are the operator values you can use:

Operator	Description
=	Equal
<	Less than
<=	Less than or equal to
>	Greater than
>=	Greater than or equal to
<>	Not equal to
BETWEEN-AND	Select a range between two values
LIKE	Search for pattern

The IN Operator

The IN Operator is used if you know the exact value you want to return for at least one of the columns.

Syntax:
SELECT "column_name"
FROM "table_name"
WHERE "column_name" IN ('value1', 'value2', ...);

The BETWEEN-AND Operator

The BETWEEN operator allows you to select a range between two values.

Syntax:
SELECT "column_name"
FROM "table_name"
WHERE "column_name" BETWEEN 'value1' AND 'value';

The LIKE Operator

LIKE operator allows you to do a search on a pattern rather than specifying exactly what is desired (as in IN) or spell out a range (as in BETWEEN).

Syntax:
SELECT "column_name"
FROM "table_name"
WHERE "column_name" LIKE 'pattern';

Pattern consists of wildcards, such as:

Wildcard	Description
A_X	All strings that start with (A)+ only one character + end with (Z). For example, (AdX) and (A9X) would both satisfy the condition, while (ADF4X) would not because there is more than one character between the (A) and (X)
%A	All strings that end with (A). For example, if you use pattern (%G) in CourseName column from the Courses table, the result will be (Marketing, Accounting)
A%	All strings that start with (A). For example, if you use pattern (J%) in StartDate column from the Courses table, the result will be (January, June)
%AN%	All strings that contain the pattern (AN) anywhere. Like Human Resources, Finance, Accounting in the courses table

The AND-OR Operator

The WHERE keyword can be a simple condition or it can be compound condition. Compound conditions are made up of multiple simple conditions connected by AND or OR.

Syntax:
SELECT "column_name"
FROM "table_name"
WHERE "column_name"
AND/OR 'simple condition';

2. SQL Data Manipulation Language (DML)

DML is used to modify data held within the database using syntax like:

- INSERT INTO – to insert new data into a database table
- UPDATE – to update data in a database table
- DELETE – to delete data from a database table

• The INSERT INTO Statement

The INSERT INTO command is used to create new data within the database. This allows you to create/insert new rows into any table (as long as you have the correct privileges).

Syntax:

INSERT INTO "table_name" (column1, column2, ...)
VALUES (value1, value2, ...) ;

• The UPDATE Statement

The UPDATE statement is used if to modify or update some data within a database table.

Syntax:

UPDATE "table_name"
SET "column_name" = "new_value"
WHERE "condition";

• The DELETE Statement

The DELETE statement is used to remove a single or multiple rows in a database table.

Syntax:

DELETE FROM "table_name"
WHERE (condition);

• TRUNCATE TABLE

This is another effective way to delete data from a table. It is a very fast way to clear out tables with many hundreds of thousands or millions rows.

Syntax:

TRUNCATE TABLE "table_name";

Note that in DELETE and TRUNCATE statements, you only remove data held in the table but you do not delete the entire table from the database. The table remains empty in the database. In the next section, the SQL DDL statements are used to remove the table from a database.

---

3. SQL Data Definition Language (DDL)

DDL is used to modify the database structure or schema. It is the part of SQL that allows you to create or delete tables. The most famous DDL statements in SQL are:

- CREATE TABLE – creates a new database table
- ALTER TABLE – changes a database table
- DROP TABLE – deletes a database table

• The CREATE TABLE Statement

The CREATE TABLE command is used to create new tables within the database.

Syntax:

CREATE TABLE "table_name"
(column_name type (size)
,column_name type (size), ...);

• The ALTER TABLE statement

This command allows you to modify or make changes in the table structure, like adding an extra column to a table:

Syntax:

ALTER TABLE "table_name"
ADD (column_name type(size));

• The DROP TABLE Statement

To entirely remove a table from the database you can use the DROP TABLE command.

Query:

DROP TABLE Members;

Note that once a table is removed, all data in this table is removed and cannot be recovered.

SQL DDL can also be used for:

- CREATE INDEX – creates an index (search key)
- DROP INDEX – deletes an index
- CREATE SYNONYM
- GRANT/REVOKE
- CREATE VIEW
- DROP VIEW
- CREATE SEQUENCE
- DROP SEQUENCE
- And others...

---

4. Querying More Than One Table

• JOINS

JOINS operation is used to query more than one table at the same time by relating tables in a database to each other with primary keys.

Syntax:

SELECT "table1_name" . "Column1name" ,
"table2_name" . "column2_name"
FROM "table1_name" . "table2_name";

• UNION

The SQL UNION command is used to combine the results of two queries together. Therefore, UNION is somewhat similar to JOIN in that they both are used to relate information from multiple tables.

Syntax:

(SQL Statement 1)
UNION
(SQL Statement 2)

• INTERSECT

Similar to the UNION command, INTERSECT also operates on two SQL statements. The difference is that, while UNION essentially acts as an OR operator, the INTERSECT command acts as an AND operator where value is selected only if it appears in table 1 and table 2.

Syntax:

(SQL Statement 1)
INTERSECT
(SQL Statement 2)

• MINUS

The MINUS operator combines the results of two or more tables and returns only data that appear in the first table after subtracting the second table. If the second table includes rows that are not present in the first table, such rows are ignored.

Syntax:

(SQL Statement 1)
MINUS
(SQL Statement 2)

---

5. Built-in Functions in SQL

Syntax:

SELECT function (column) FROM table;

7

Introduction to Lean Six Sigma

I. Lean Six Sigma

Lean Six Sigma knowledge area represents the third dimension of the 3D Business Analyst. Much of the business analysis work is about improving the process implemented by considering a problem, finding the root cause(s), developing alternative solutions and recommending the best resolution for the situation. Improving decision making at all levels of an organization enhances the short and long-term performance of the business. 3D business analysts are strategic decision makers.

Poor decisions can lead to decreases in productivity and increases in waste. In Corporate America it is clearer than ever that lean process is the single most powerful tool available for creating value while eliminating waste in any organization.

In this chapter you will learn the power of Lean Six Sigma, the lean principles, the five phases of the DMAIC process, and understand the basic Lean Six Sigma tool set.

Firstly, you need to understand what Lean is, what Six Sigma is, and why and how to integrate to Lean Six Sigma.

	I. Lean	II. Six Sigma	III. Integration
Focus	Eliminate Waste	Eliminate Variation	Eliminate waste with highest quality
Goal	Add value to customer	Improve quality	Zero errors
Principles	1. Value 2. The Value Stream 3. Flow 4. Pull 5. Perfection	DMAIC: 1. Define 2. Measure 3. Analyze 4. Improve 5. Control	(see the integration section)

I. Lean Process

Lean process is the framework used to eliminate waste in a process (convert waste into value). It is called Lean because it offers a methodology to produce more with less human effort, less equipment, less time, less space, while providing customers with exactly what they want. Sounds ideal right? Let's see how this can be done!

- Lean process creates new jobs rather than destroying jobs in the name of efficiency.

What is Waste (*Muda*)?

Muda is a Japanese word for "waste". It basically represents anyone, anything, or any activity that absorbs enterprise resources but creates no value from the customer's perspective.
In Lean process, there are 8 types of wastes:

1. **Transportation:** unnecessary transportations could be stakeholders, equipment, or documents between office locations

2. **Inventory:** could be excess paperwork in your office, work in progress, or equipment that is holding space

3. **Motion:** it's the movement of employees with no purpose, like walking to get tools or to the copy machine, or looking for people (example, figure 7-6)

4. **Waiting:** a group of people in a downstream activity standing around waiting because an upstream activity has not delivered on time, like waiting for information or approvals from stakeholders could hold up the technical team from starting their system design

5. **Overproduction:** production of items that is not needed, like adding requirements not requested by the clients (gold plating) or excessive or unread reports, etc.

6. **Excess processing:** too many processing steps that are not actually needed, like too many inspections, work redundancy and multiple document drafts

7. **Defects:** mistakes which require rework or change requests

8. **Non-utilized talent:** like not inviting the appropriate stakeholders to your meetings

- Now that the wastes are defined for you, change your perspective and make it a habit to observe any wastes in your day to day activities and work on improving them.

Principles of Lean Process:

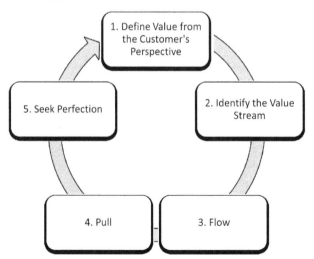

Figure 7-1

Lean production is a strategy that uses less of everything compared to traditional manufacturing. The focus is on eliminating waste or non-value added activities within a process.

1. Define Value

Value is defined from the customer's perspective in terms of goals, needs and requirements. This is called "Voice Of Customer (VOC)". It is any feature or step in the process that the customer has requested, and is willing to pay for if done right the first time – the customer will not pay twice for the same product.

Various tools are used to define the Voice Of Customer (VOC):
- Interviews
- Focus Groups
- Questionnaires and Surveys
- JAD Sessions
- Brainstorming
- Complaints
- Root-Cause Analysis (Fishbone Diagram)
- Kano model – to analyze customer requirements
- Quality Function Deployment (QFD)

Most of these tools are explained in the requirements elicitation tools in chapter 3. Now let's add 2 more elicitation tools to your skill set:

Kano Model

This model was created by Noriaki Kano. It categorizes the customer needs into 3 main categories:

1. <u>Must Be's or Dissatisfiers:</u> they represent the basic requirements that the customer is expecting as part of the solution. If these requirements are not present, the customer will be dissatisfied. For example, when you purchase a car you expect to drive it to work (basic need)

2. <u>More is Better or Satisfiers:</u> they are requirements that the more is met the better. Like having a cup holder in your new car or cell phone features, if they are present you will be satisfied

3. <u>Delighters:</u> they are features that exceed the customer expectations. Imagine meeting the customer expectations with the basic needs and satisfiers requirements and exceeding that with a life time guarantee. This would be a delighter!

Note that competition in today's markets raises the basic expectations of customers. The standards of a happy customer continue to rise. What was once considered a delighter, may in time turn into a basic need.

- We discussed prioritizing requirements in chapter-3, now you know that this is also called Kano model.

Quality Function Deployment (QFD)

QFD is an example of a facilitated workshop technique that ensures that the customers' needs and requirements are heard and translated into technical characteristics for new solution development. QFD starts by collecting customer needs, also known as voice of the customer (VOC). These needs are then objectively sorted and prioritized, and goals are set for achieving them.

QFD diagram in figure 7-2 is also called "house of quality", which is a technique used to organize the data. It is a matrix that represents the relationship between the customer needs and the design features and requirements.

House of Quality - QFD

Correlation

How vs Hows

How to meet the customer
requirements?
(Design Features)
(HOWs)

| Customer Requirements (WHATs) (VOC) | Relationship Matrix (How vs. What) | Comparison of customer priorities (WHY) |

Benchmarked

Or

Target Values

Figure 7-2

To depict a detailed solution design, Hauser (1988) suggests using the "hows" from one house of quality as the "whats" of another house. (see figure 7-3)

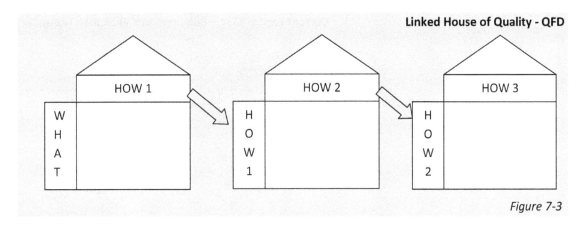

Figure 7-3

2. Identify Value Stream

The *value stream* is the entire set of tasks (activities) required to create a specific product from requirements to its final state presented to the end user. Identifying the value stream of your project will allow you to realize the gap between the value stream (ideal stream) and the current stream in your organization. Many of the activities in the current stream could be eliminated almost immediately with dramatic cost savings.

Process mapping tools described in chapter-5 are used to create:
- <u>Current state map:</u> which is the process exactly as it occurs now, not how it is supposed to or how you wish or think it should occur
- <u>Ideal state map:</u> it is the value stream. The benefits of identifying the ideal state before thinking about the future state is that the ideal state shifts the entire paradigm for the team, so they think about what they want to achieve instead of focusing on fixing mistakes in the current map
- <u>Future state</u> is the improved flow that we want to achieve based on using LEAN tools and methodologies. The future state is not created in this phase, usually it is created after incorporating the lean principles of Flow and Pull (after the analysis work is done)

- When identifying the current state, remember the rule of three actuals: capture the <u>actual</u> work done by talking to the <u>actual</u> person performing it in the <u>actual</u> place it is happening!

Now let's assume there is a project to improve the "requirements elicitation" process. Create a current state (As-Is) of the three major mapping diagrams:
a) **Logical map:** it is the process flow map, like activity and sequence diagrams to depict how the process flows from start to end. Logical map makes it easy to study handoffs between parties in a process (explained in chapter 5)

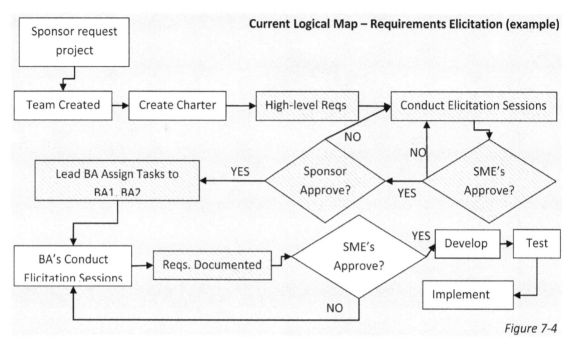

Figure 7-4

In figure 7-4, the logical map represents the current flow of the software development process from start to end. Certainly there are several wastes to be eliminated from the process, to do that we need to create the Value Stream (Ideal State) to identify the crucial steps that cannot be eliminated.

- Think LEAN, always look for wastes and work on eliminating them

Let's think of the sponsor, one of your customers. What would add value to the customer in this process? In other words, what would the sponsor care about? If you ask the sponsor, his/her words will be, "I want my requirements to be developed, tested for errors and implemented on my system". That's true, that's what adds value to the customer! Then the Ideal State is as follows:

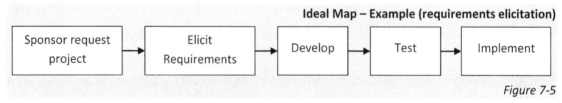

Figure 7-5

So now the goal is to incorporate the lean principles of Pull and Flow to create a future state map that is as close as possible to the ideal map.

b) **Physical map:** it represents the physical flow of information, materials, documents between different steps and parties

How to draw Physical Map
- Use floor plans (one or multiple) for actual physical locations or draw a workplace layout
- Draw icon to represent offsite locations
- Draw a line for every physical trip (from and to each party). For example if the PM takes 3 trips to the Lead BA and the Lead BA takes 2 trips to the PM, that's a total of 5 lines (see figure 7-6)

Draw a physical map of the team flow in the same requirements elicitation process:

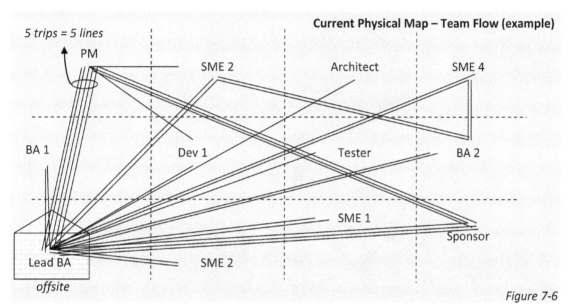

Figure 7-6

In the example, the physical map shows movement and transportation activities performed by the team members to communicate with each other. It shows all trips carried out by each party. For example, the sponsor has completed 6 trips (3 to the PM + 3 to the Lead BA, who is located offsite). That's a total of 6 lines on the map.

In figure 7-6, by analyzing the physical map you can notice that the physical location of the team members needs to be re-assigned to its optimum way. For example, from the map you can tell that the Lead BA is a very critical member in the team and the need to communicate with him/her is wasting the team's time, money and probably affecting their performance. This is a kind of *motion and transportation* wastes that you will need to work on in the next step (FLOW) to improve the physical layout of the work place.

c) **Functional map (spaghetti diagram):** it is pretty much the same concept as the physical map but it depicts the functional flow instead of the physical flow.

How to draw physical and functional maps
- Draw a circle and add all parties involved on it like in figure 7-7

- Draw lines from each sender to each receiver
- Same as the physical map, draw a line for each functional communication (could be requirements elicitation, review, inquiries, approvals, etc.)
- Identify bottlenecks – you will have more than one bottleneck in more complex projects

Let's see the same example:

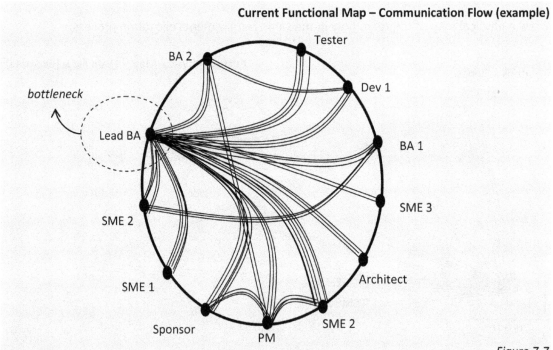

Current Functional Map – Communication Flow (example)

Figure 7-7

Functional maps show how information flows between team members, like who talks to whom and how many times regardless of their physical location.

In figure 7-7, by analyzing the functional map you can obviously determine the Lead BA is a bottleneck in the flow of information in this process, which could have consequences on the project schedule, cost, and performance. Again, in the next step (FLOW) you will work on relieving bottlenecks by offloading, better prioritization, re-engineering the process, etc.

3. Flow (make the process flow)

Once value has been accurately defined, the value stream for the product is completely mapped as well as the current state and bottlenecks have been identified, it is time for the next step in lean process: Eliminate the wasteful steps in the process that is causing the bottlenecks to make the process flow.

- What flows in software industry? Information, documents, requirements, approvals, etc.
- The goal is to make the system flow as smooth and easy as possible by eliminating constraints and bottlenecks.

4. Pull

Pull is a method of work where nothing is produced by a downstream workstation unless an upstream work station triggers a need.

Now let's apply FLOW and PULL principles to eliminate wastes and relieve bottlenecks from the process and create a future state map:

NOTE THAT ALL DIAGRAMS AND ANALYSIS WORK IS PERFORMED BY THE PROCESS IMPROVEMENT TEAM. YOU WILL NOT BE REQUIRED TO DO ANY OF THAT AS A BUSINESS ANALYST. THE PURPOSE OF THIS CHAPTER IS TO LEARN – AS A 3D BUSINESS ANALYST – TO CHANGE YOUR PERSPECTIVE AND THINK LEAN!!

For now, let's assume the highlighted activities in figure 7-4 are wastes because they consume a lot of time and do not add value to the customer (this is decided by brainstorming with the team, will be explained in the six sigma section). Then Future Logical Map would be as follows in figure 7-8:

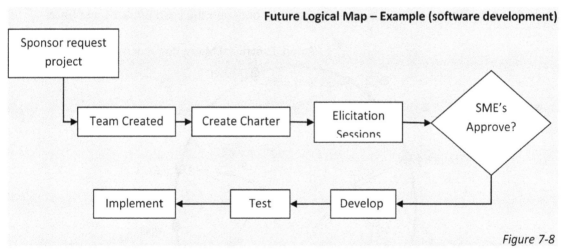

Future Logical Map – Example (software development)

Figure 7-8

To eliminate the motion and transportation wasted on communication with the Lead BA we need to relieve the bottleneck identified. Some solutions to relieve the bottleneck at the Lead BA could be:

1. Relocate the Lead BA to work onsite
2. Place the Lead BA in the center of the work place to be reachable by all team members
3. Reassign tasks between Lead BA, BA 1 and BA 2

---

4. Relocate other team members' physical location to more efficient locations based on their communication needs

5. Apply PULL principle to reduce communication with SME's (BA's pull information when needed)

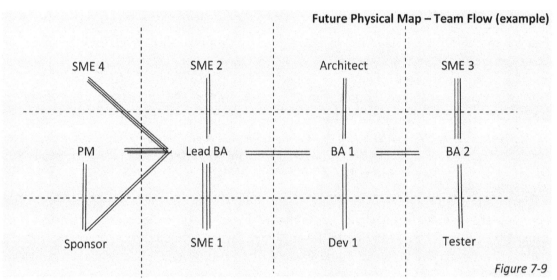

Figure 7-9

Now let's create the future state of the functional map. Remember that our goal is to eliminate wastes and relieve bottlenecks by reassigning tasks between the Lead BA, BA 1 and BA 2.

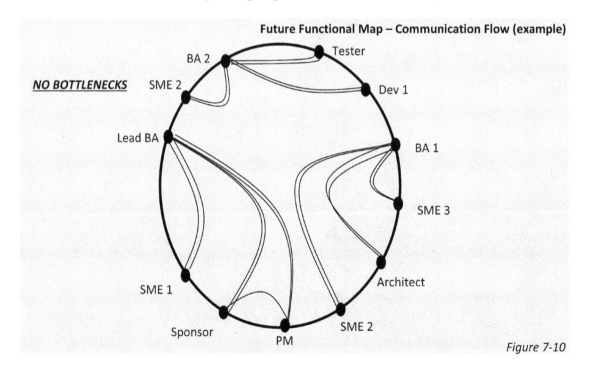

Figure 7-10

AGAIN, THIS IS JUST AN EXAMPLE TO SHOW HOW LEAN PRINCIPLES ARE APPLIED INTO A PRO-CESS TO ELIMINATE WASTES.THIS DOES NOT MEAN THAT THE ELIMINATED ACTIVITIES ARE AC-TUAL WASTE, THE PURPOSE IS TO SHOW HOW LEAN THINKING MAKES DIFFERENCES BETWEEN CURRENT AND FUTURE MAPPING DIAGRAMS!

5. Seek Perfection

Perfection state is reaching to a system that contains absolutely no waste, so that every activity along the process stream adds value to the customer.

- Perfection means keep looking for waste and eliminate them
- Perfection is a never ending journey, not a destination
- There is no end to the process of reducing effort, time, space, cost, and mistakes (Kaizen)

Tools for perfection are:
- Lean thinking: lean activities are a cycle of never ending process (figure 7-1)
- Mistake proofing: by performing regular quality inspections to ensure defects cannot be created
- Leadership: organization leadership must support the Lean thinking process
- Six Sigma: ensuring zero errors (this will be explained in the very next page)

Demonstrated benefits of becoming LEAN
- Improve product quality
- Flexibility in responding to changes
- Reduce cost
- Increase on-time delivery (no missed deadlines)
- Continuously improve cost, schedule and quality

BUILD UP YOUR LEAN PROCESS VOCABULARY

- Bottleneck: it is a resource whose capacity is equal to or less than the demand placed upon it. In other words, it is the slowest activity within a process. The goal is to relieve bottlenecks

- Business Non-Value Added: the time needed to perform activities that are required to create a product but the customer would not pay for (like team status reporting)

- Customer: someone for whom the work is performed. As a business analyst, your customer would be anyone using your deliverables in a downstream work process like developers, testers, project managers, SME's, end users, etc

- Customer Value Add: time required to perform an activity that changes the form, look or function of a product to meet the needs of the customer

- Muda: Japanese word for waste

- Rework: non-value add work performed to correct a defect that has occurred

- Throughput: the rate at which the system generates money through sales

- WIP: Work In Progress

- WIIFM: What's In It For Me? A term used to get the organization's staff buy-in to your process improvement project. You explain to them what's in this project for them

II. Six Sigma (6σ)

"Six sigma has forever changed GE (General Electric). Everyone is a true believer in Six Sigma, the way this company works now". (John F. Welch, Former GE Chairman)

Six sigma is a highly structured process that focuses on developing and delivering products and services with zero errors (near-perfect).

So what is Sigma (σ)? And why "six" sigma (6σ)?

Sigma is a statistical term that represents that standard deviation of a process about its mean. Standard deviation is used to measure how widely spread the data values are compared to the mean. If standard deviation (σ) is zero, this means that all data values are equal and there is no error (no variation) in the process. This is the ideal case.

- Sigma (σ) is a measure of <u>variation</u> for process performance
- It provides information about the amount of variation in a process

In normally distributed process:
- A 1σ process has a yield (productivity) of = 68% and defect or error rate = 32%
- 3σ = 99.73% yield, defect = 0.027%
- 4σ = 9939968%
- 6σ = 99.9999998% yield!!!

You might ask why we need to go all the way to 6σ when 3σ provides us a yield of 99.73%? Well, let's see how good a 3σ (99.73%) process is?

A process that provides 99.73% certainty would result in:
- 21,000 incorrect drug prescriptions annually
- 110 mistaken medical procedures daily
- More than 2 million documents lost by IRS annually
- 18,000 pieces of mishandled mail per hour
- 33 plane accidents per million flights

Let's see the defects rate per million opportunities (DPMO) for each σ process: (The failure rate can also be referred to as Defects Per Opportunity (DPO)

Sigma Level	DPMO
6σ	3.4
5σ	233
4σ	6,210
3σ	66,810
2σ	305,538
1σ	691,462

So you apply the sigma level that is appropriate to your process. Of course 6σ is the safest choice, but has a huge cost impact to move from one sigma level to a higher one. An average company applies 3σ process.

The six sigma process steps are described as DMAIC:

DMAIC is a structured problem-solving framework widely used in six sigma process. It consists of five phases: **D**efine, **M**easure, **A**nalyze, **I**mprove, and **C**ontrol.

- DMAIC is pronounced as "Duh-MAY-ick"
- DMAIC framework supports creative thinking within the system boundaries, i.e., keeps basic processes, products or services. It does not start a new system from scratch.

Define ⇨ Measure ⇨ Analyze ⇨ Improve ⇨ Control

Figure 7-11

1. Define (customer & goals to understand problem)

Process Improvement projects start with a need or a goal to be achieved. In the define phase, team members get introduced to the project, their roles and what they are trying to achieve.

- The define phase in DMAIC is very similar in concept to the initiation phase in project management explained in Chapter 2.

Tools and tasks performed in define stage:
- Define the project goals (why are you doing the project?)
- Create the project charter (what is the problem, goals, scope, schedule, impact, and team?)
- Develop the team and launch the project

- Define the customer
- Define value from customer's perspective, "Voice Of Customer" *(Lean & Six Sigma integration)*
- Develop SIPOC Diagram

All of these tools and tasks you are already familiar with and have been explained in previous chapters in this book. SIPOC is a new tool for you to add to your skill set.

So what is SIPOC? It is a process used to describe the process <u>S</u>upplier – <u>I</u>nput – <u>P</u>rocess – <u>O</u>utput – <u>C</u>ustomer. SIPOC allows the team of identify the project scope and agree on its boundaries. It is also a great tool to verify that the process inputs match outputs of the preceding (upstream) process and inputs/expectations of the successive (downstream) process.

- Supplier: could be internal or external supplier to the process
- Inputs: could be material, documents, information, requirements, etc
- Process: a block representing the entire process to produce the output
- Outputs: deliverables or work products
- Customer: could be internal or external customers depends on the process scope

Note that the customer does not necessarily have to be the end user or an outsider. The customer is any person or organization that directly receives an output from work activity. So let's create a SIPOC diagram for the "requirement elicitation process" example: (this is actually very useful for your BA role to identify your customers and know their expectations)

SIPOC Diagram – Requirements Elicitation (example)

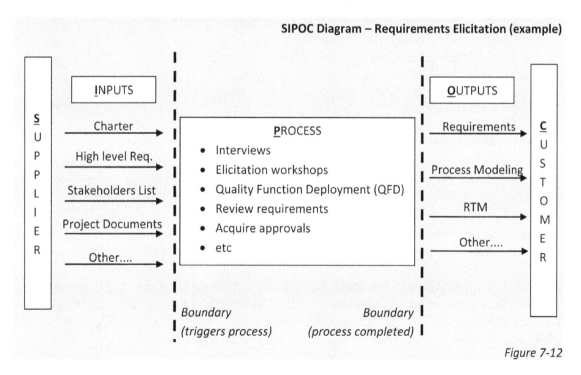

Figure 7-12

In this example, suppliers are: domain experts, stakeholders, technical team, testing team and end user because they supply the BA with information used to create the outputs. To identify customers, ask yourself who has interest in your deliverables. Development team will use your requirements to code the system, testing team will create test cases using your documents, business owners and domain experts need to approve your documents. There you go, you just defined your process, what you need to start, what is expected from you by whom and who supplies you with your needs.

- A SIPOC can be created in any order; however, it is recommended to identify the Process, followed by Customer, Outputs, Inputs, and then suppliers.

2. Measure (where are we now?)

The work you have done in the Define stage is to understand the process required to improve its performance and identify the customer goals. In the Measure stage you need to clarify things by investigating how and how well the work gets done. The purpose is to establish the current performance level (baseline) and collect data about the process to be analyzed in the next stage. Tools and tasks performed in the Measure stage:

- Walk the process
- Collect baseline data
- Create current logical map *(Lean & Six Sigma integration)*
- Create current physical and functional maps *(Lean & Six Sigma integration)*
- Identify problems and opportunities
- Other statistical tools

Again, when you are collecting data about the process use the 3 Actuals rule.

3. Analyze (understand why problems occur)

Now that you know what is happening in your process, it is time to find out why and identify the potential root causes of the problem, which you will work on resolving and improving in the next stage.

Root-cause analysis (Fish-bone diagram) and 5 Whys technique are the most common tools used to push the team beyond symptoms to uncover potential root causes. (Explained in Chapter 3)

Both Measure and Analyze stages involve a good amount of advanced tools that require more in-depth knowledge of statistical principles which will not be covered in this book, as this is an introduction to Lean Six Sigma. However, here are the common tools used to measure and analyze the process performance for your further readings:

- Measurement System Analysis
- System Capabilities Cp & Cpк
- Regression Analysis
- Failure Modes & Effects Analysis (FMEA)
- Control Charts
- Hypothesis Testing
- 5S Technique – *see the 6σ vocabulary section*
- Theory Of Constraints (TOC)
- Analysis Of Variance (ANOVA)
- Time Value Analysis

see the 6σ vocabulary section

4. Improve (Solve problems)

At this point, you have <u>defined</u> your customers and their goals, <u>measured</u> your process to understand its current state, and performed further <u>analysis</u> on the system to identify the root causes of the process problems. Now it is time to brainstorm with the team to come up with some ideas to address the root causes, select the best ones and implement them to <u>improve</u> the process.

Tools and tasks performed in the Improve stage:
- Develop the ideal state map *(Lean & Six Sigma integration)*
- Use Lean principles (FLOW & PULL) to eliminate waste *(Lean & Six Sigma integration)*
- Brainstorm improvement ideas
- Prioritize and select improvement ideas by using PICK Chart
- Develop Future State Maps *(Lean & Six Sigma integration)*
- Design Of Experiments (DOE)

What is a PICK Chart? After brainstorming is completed, you will have a lot of improvement ideas (could be hundreds) that need to be evaluated. PICK Chart is a great tool to evaluate and prioritize ideas in order to select the best improvement solutions to apply to your process.

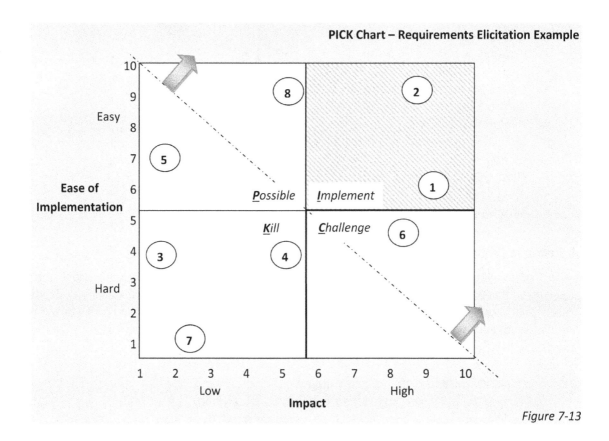

Figure 7-13

PICK is an acronym for Possible – Implement – Challenge – Kill. Draw the PICK Chart and add ideas to it based on how easy they are to implement and their impact to improve the process. Start implementing ideas that fall in the implement box (shaded) then ideas that are above the dotted line. Ideas that fall in the Kill box are killed and not considered because they are hard to implement with low impact on the process. Let's see how to use the PICK Chart on the "requirements elicitation" example.

Let's assume you have the following ideas to improve the current physical map for the "requirements elicitation" example (figure 7-6):

1. Relocate the Lead BA to work onsite
2. Reassign tasks between Lead BA, BA1 and BA2
3. Hire an additional PM
4. Hire an additional BA
5. Train BA's on requirements elicitation
6. Re-structure the workplace to make team members more reachable to each other based on their communication needs

7. Purchase more advanced computers

8. Apply PULL principle to reduce communication with SME's (BA's pull information from team members only when needed)

Now put the ideas on the PICK Chart as in figure 8-12. Start with implementing ideas 1, 2 then 4, 6. Ideas 3, 4, 5 and 7 should be killed because they are hard to implement and have very low impact.

After implementing selected ideas, develop future state maps for the process *(see figures 8-9 & 8-10)*. Then design a set of structured tests to measure and assess the effect of these changes on the process. This is called Design Of Experiments.

Design Of Experiments (DOE) is a systematic approach to investigate a process. It is a more advanced technique than the classical experiments that tends to change only one factor at a time and hold everything else constant (impossible to do in a complicated process). DOE can focus on a wide range of key input factors or variables, making the DOE process economical and less interruptive.

5. Control (sustain achievements)

In this stage you need to control the process to make sure to sustain what you have achieved in process improvements. Putting a control plan in place is crucial to ensure that the process is carried out consistently and it does not go back to its initial state before improvements. Also controlling the process will result in early detection of any defects that could occur later on.

Tools and tasks performed in the Control stage:
- Measurement System Analysis (MSA): it is the process of validating and calibrating the measurement system for its accuracy, sensitivity and precision
- Control Chart: it is a time plot chart showing process performance, mean (average) and control limits. It is used to determine if the process is in control (within control limits) or not.
- Communication Plan (explained in Chapter 3)
- Target Progress Report
- Sustainment Plan
- Transitioning the project to the customer and closing it

What is Target Progress Report? It is a report presented to the customer or management at the end of the project showing the improvement percentage to the process, such as:

Goals	Current	Future	% Improvement
List the goals defined by the customer in the define stage	*What is the current state*	*What is the future state after implementing improvements?*	*Measure the improvement percentage (e.g. 60% reduced time, cost reduced by 50%, etc.*

BUILD UP YOUR SIX SIGMA VOCABULARY

- 5S Technique: It is a process of creating and maintaining a structured, clean and high performance workplace. The 5 – S's are Sort, Set in order, Shine, Standardize, and Sustain.

- Analysis Of Variance (ANOVA): It is a basic statistical technique for analyzing experimental data. It subdivides the total variation of a data set into meaningful component parts associated with specific sources of variation in order to test a hypothesis on the parameters of the model or to estimate variance components. There are three models: fixed, random, and mixed.

- Benchmarking: An improvement process in which a company measures its performance against that of best-in-class companies, determines how those companies achieved their performance levels, and uses the information to improve its own performance. The subjects that can be benchmarked include strategies, operations, processes, and procedures.

- Brainstorming: A technique that teams use to generate ideas on a particular subject. Each person in the team is asked to think creatively and write down as many ideas as possible. The ideas are not discussed or reviewed until after the brainstorming session.

- Capability: A measure of quality for a process usually expressed as sigma capability, Cpk, or defects per million opportunities (DPMO). It is obtained by comparing the actual process with the specification limits.

- Corrective Action: The implementation of solutions resulting in the reduction or elimination of an identified problem.

- Cost of Poor Quality: The costs associated with providing poor-quality products or services. There are four categories of costs: internal failure costs (costs associated with defects found before the customer receives the product or service), external failure costs (costs associated with defects found after the customer receives the product or service), appraisal costs (costs incurred to determine the degree of conformance to quality requirements), and prevention costs (costs incurred to keep failure and appraisal costs to a minimum).

- Defect Prevention: Any attempt at eliminating the root cause of defects prior to their occurrence.

- Efficiency: The ratio of the actual product produced to a standard. Calculated by dividing the standard parts per hour by the actual parts per hour.

- Failure Mode Effect Analysis (FMEA): A procedure in which each potential failure mode in every sub- item of an item is analyzed to determine its effect on other sub-items and on the required function of the item.

- Just-In-Time (JIT): A manufacturing practice pioneered by the Toyota Motor Company where each workstation acquires the required materials from upstream workstations precisely as needed. JIT requires a systems approach to transforming the manufacturing environment and is focused on continuous improvement.

BUILD UP YOUR SIX SIGMA VOCABULARY

- Kaizen: A Japanese term that means continuous improvement of a process to create value with less Muda. This is done by doing little things better and setting and achieving increasingly higher standards.

- Kaikaku: A Japanese term that means radical improvement of a process to eliminate Muda.

- Mean: The average of a set of values.

- Median: For a sample the number that is in the middle when all observations are ranked in magnitude.

- Nominal Group Technique (NGT): A technique, similar to brainstorming, used by teams to generate ideas on a particular subject. Team members are asked to silently come up with as many ideas as possible, writing them down. Each member is then asked to share one idea, which is recorded. After all the ideas are recorded, they are discussed and prioritized by the group.

- Pareto Principle: 80% of the trouble comes from 20% of the problems.

- Probability: A measure of the likelihood of a given event occurring.

- Regression: A statistical technique for determining the best mathematical expression describing the functional relationship between one response and one or more independent variables.

- Sample: A group of units or observations taken from a larger collection to provide information that may be used as a basis for making a decision concerning the larger quantity.

- Sigma: A Greek letter that is often used to describe the standard deviation of data.

- Standard Deviation (S or σ): A mathematical quantity that describes the variability of a response. It equals the square root of variance. The standard deviation of a sample (S) is used to estimate the standard deviation of a population (σ).

- Variance: A measure of variability in a data set or population. It is the square of the standard deviation.

- Variation: A change in data, a characteristic, or a function that is caused by one of four factors: special causes, common causes, tampering, or structural variation.

- Tampering: Action taken to compensate for variation within the control limits of a stable system. Tampering increases rather than decreases variation.

III. Integration

About eight years ago, books published on the integration use of Lean and Six Sigma were almost nonexistent. In today's libraries, integration represents more than one-half of the Lean books and almost 30% of the Six Sigma books.

There has been an ongoing debate regarding the difference between Lean and Six Sigma, and whether they should be implemented independently. Lean tools are about eliminating wastes and creating a better flow to reduce a process cycle time. Six Sigma brings a process under control to eliminate defects and improve quality. So both Lean and Six Sigma are complementary tool sets not competing philosophies, where they focus heavily on satisfying customers and they both empower people to create process stability and a culture of continuous improvement.

Many tools and techniques are commonly used by both lean and six sigma methodologies. Such as, brainstorming, PICK Chart, cause-and-effect diagrams, 5 "whys", and others.

Benefits of integration (Lean and Six Sigma marriage):
- Lean provides stability to a process
- When stability is achieved, variation due to human defects goes away
- Data collected in DMAIC framework (Measure stage) is utilized in the lean process
- Respond to customers faster, with less waste and higher quality
- Combine time-based strategy (Lean) with organizational process and analytical tools (6σ)

For example, if a Lean specific projects represent a 10% improvement over time, and Six Sigma initiatives represent another 10%, then an integration could potentially represent and improvement of 20%. See figure 7-14.

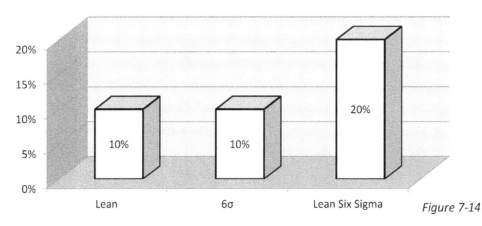

Lean and Six Sigma Integration

Figure 7-14

Lean Six Sigma is not just for manufacturing processes. All processes can and should be attacked using Lean Six Sigma tools, such as:

- Customer facing processes like call centers
- Reservations and ordering
- Transportation and delivery
- Health care and medical treatment
- Internal business processes like the elicitation requirements process we used in this chapter
- Hiring and training process

Problem focus for Lean Six Sigma:

- Improve quality, such as:
  - Incorrect information *(wrong or missed requirements)*
  - Incorrect execution *(requirements documented but not developed)*
  - Simpler process *(easier flow)*
  - More flexible process *(have it your way)*
- Reduce cycle time, such as:
  - Faster requirements gathering
  - Faster decision making
  - Faster development
  - Faster testing

I. Lean / II. Six Sigma (comparison)

	I. Lean	II. Six Sigma
Focus	Eliminate Waste	Eliminate Variation
Goal	Add value to customer	Improve quality
Principles	1. Value 2. The Value Stream 3. Flow 4. Pull 5. Perfection	DMAIC: 1. **D**efine 2. **M**easure 3. **A**nalyze 4. **I**mprove 5. **C**ontrol

I. Lean Process

Lean process is the framework used to eliminate waste in a process (convert waste into value). It is called Lean because it offers a methodology to produce more with less human effort, less equipment, less time, less space, while providing customers with exactly what they want.

- **What is Waste (Muda)?**

Muda is a Japanese word for "waste". It basically represents anyone, anything, or any activity that absorbs enterprise resources but creates no value from the customer's perspective.

In Lean process, there are 8 types of wastes:

1. Transportation
2. Overproduction
3. Inventory
4. Excess processing
5. Motion
6. Defects
7. Waiting
8. Non-utilized talent

- **Principles of Lean Process:**

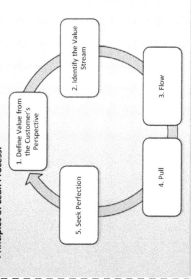

1. Define Value

Value is defined from the customer's perspective in terms of goals, needs and requirements. This is called "Voice Of Customer (VOC)". It is any feature or step in the process that the customer has requested, and is willing to pay for if done right the first time – the customer will not pay twice for the same product.

2. Identify Value Stream

The value stream is the entire set of tasks (activities) required to create a specific product from requirements to its final state presented to the end user. Identifying the value stream of your project will allow you to realize the gap between the value stream (ideal stream) and the current stream in your organization. Many of the activities in the current stream could be eliminated almost immediately with dramatic cost savings.

3. Flow (make the process flow)

Once value has been accurately defined, the value stream for the product is completely mapped as well as the current state and bottlenecks have been identified, it is time for the next step in lean process: Eliminate the wasteful steps in the process that is causing the bottlenecks to make the process flow.

4. Pull

Pull is a method of work where nothing is produced by a downstream workstation unless an upstream work station triggers a need.

5. Seek Perfection

Perfection state is reaching to a system that contains absolutely no waste, so that every activity along the process stream adds value to the customer.

Demonstrated benefits of becoming LEAN

- Improve product quality
- Flexibility in responding to changes
- Reduce cost
- Increase on-time delivery (no missed deadlines)
- Continuously improve cost, schedule and quality

II. Six Sigma (6σ)

Six sigma is a highly structured process that focuses on developing and delivering products and services with zero errors (near-perfect).

In normally distributed process:

- A 1σ process has a yield (productivity) of = 68% and defect or error rate = 32%
- 3σ = 99.73% yield, defect = 0.027%
- 4σ = 9939968%
- 6σ = 99.9999998% yield!!!

Defect Per Million Opportunity (DPMO):

Sigma Level	DPMO
6σ	3.4
5σ	233
4σ	6,210
3σ	66,810
2σ	305,538
1σ	691,462

- **The six sigma process steps are described as DMAIC:**

DMAIC is a structured problem-solving framework widely used in six sigma process. It consists of five phases: **D**efine, **M**easure, **A**nalyze, **I**mprove, and **C**ontrol.

Define ⇨ Measure ⇨ Analyze ⇨ Improve ⇨ Control

1. Define (customer & goals to understand problem)

Process Improvement projects start with a need or a goal to be achieved. In the define phase, team members get introduced to the project, their roles and what they are trying to achieve.

2. Measure (where are we now?)

The work you have done in the Define stage is to understand the process required to improve its performance and identify the customer goals. In the Measure stage you need to clarify things by investigating how and how well the work gets done. The purpose is to establish the current performance level (baseline) and collect data about the process to be analyzed in the next stage.

3. Analyze (understand why problems occur)

Now that you know what is happening in your process, it is time to find out why and identify the potential root causes of the problem, which you will work on resolving and improving in the next stage.

4. Improve (Solve problems)

At this point, you have defined your customers and their goals, measured your process to understand its current state, and performed further analysis on the system to identify the root causes of the process problems. Now it is time to brainstorm with the team to come up with some ideas to address the root causes, select the best ones and implement them to improve the process.

5. Control (sustain achievements)

In this stage you need to control the process to make sure to sustain what you have achieved in process improvements. Putting a control plan in place is crucial to ensure that the process is carried out consistently and it does not go back to its initial state before improvements. Also controlling the process will result in early detection of any defects that could occur later on.

III. Integration

Benefits of integration (Lean and Six Sigma marriage):

○ Lean provides stability to a process
○ When stability is achieved, variation due to human defects goes away
○ Data collected in DMAIC framework (Measure stage) is utilized in the lean process
○ Respond to customers faster, with less waste and higher quality
○ Combine time-based strategy (Lean) with organizational process and analytical tools (6σ)

8

Templates

Project Charter

Project Title/Name: _____

Project Sponsor: _____ **Date Prepared:** _____

Project Manager: _____ **Customer:** _____

Project Purpose or Justification

Define the reason the project is being undertaken. This section may refer to a business case, the organization's strategic plan, external factors, a contract or any other document or reason for performing the project.

Project Description

Provide a summary-level description of the project. This section may include information on high-level product and project deliverables as well as the approach to the project.

High-level Project and Product Requirements

Define the high-level conditions or capabilities that must be met to satisfy the purpose of the project. Describe the product features and functions that must be present to meet stakeholders' needs and expectations. This section does not describe the detailed requirements as those are covered in requirements documentation.

Summary Budget

List the initial range of estimated expenditures for the project.

Initial Risks

Document initial project risks, these will later be entered into a Risk Register when project planning begins.

Success Criteria

The specific and measureable criteria that will determine project success.

Acceptance Criteria

The minimum criteria that must be met so that customer or sponsor accepts the project.

Summary Milestones	Due Date
List the significant events in the project. These can include the completion of key deliverables, the beginning or completion of a project phase or product acceptance.	*Completion date of the milestone.*

Project Manager Authority Level

- *Staffing decisions – define the authority of the project manager to select, hire, fire, discipline, accept or not accept project staff.*
- *Budget management – define the authority of the project manager to commit, manage, and control project funds.*
- *Conflict resolution - define the authority of the project manager to resolve conflict within the team, within the organization, and with external stakeholders.*
- *Escalation path for authority limitations – define the path of escalation for issues outside the authority level of the project manager.*
- *Technical decisions – define the authority of the project manager to make technical decisions about the deliverables or the project approach.*

Approvals

Project Manager's Signature   Sponsor's Signature

Project Manager's Name   Sponsor's Name

Date   Date

Work Breakdown Structure (WBS)

Project Title:————————————————————————

Date Prepared:————————————————————————

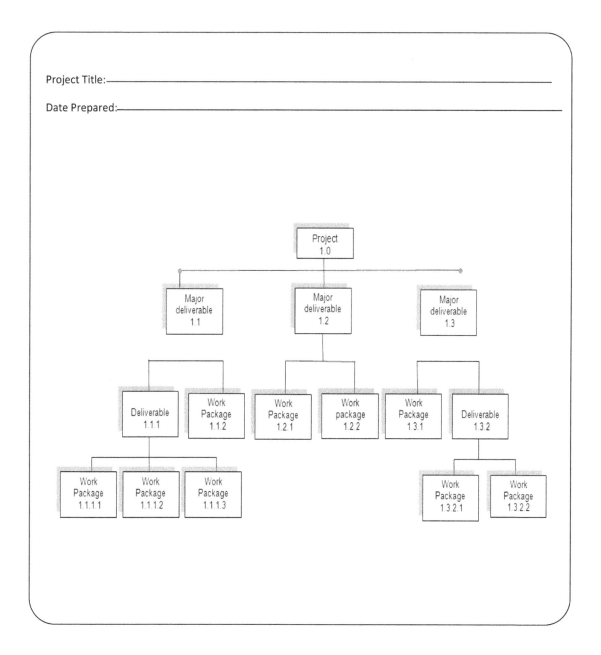

Change Management Plan

Project Title:———————————————— **Date Prepared:**————————————————

Change Management Approach

Discussed in the project management for BA chapter.

Definition of Change

Schedule Change
Budget Change
Scope Change
Project Document Changes

Change Control Board (CCB)

Name	Role	Responsibility	Authority

Change Control Process

Change request submittal	
Change request tracking	
Change request review	
Change request disposition	

Note: Attach relevant forms used in the change control process

Change Request (CR)

Project Title: ————————————   **Date Prepared:** ————————————

Stakeholder Requesting Change:—————   **CR Name:** ————————————

CR Creator: ————————————   **CR Number:** ————————————

Category of Change

- ☐ Scope
- ☐ Cost
- ☐ Quality
- ☐ Schedule
- ☐ Requirements
- ☐ Documents

Priority   ☐ High (red)   ☐ Medium (yellow)   ☐ Low (green)

Change Description

What is the change requested?

e.g., add a log in functionality to access the company's directory.

Justification/Reason for Change

Why do we need this change? Is it worth implementing?

e.g., business owner needs a log in functionality for security to provide access to certain people.

Impact of Change

What is the change impact on the following:
- *Scope*
- *Requirements*
- *Schedule*
- *Budget*
- *Quality*

Disposition   ☐ Approved   ☐ Defer   ☐ Reject

Change Control Board Signatures

Name	Role	Signature

Project Scope Statement

Project Title: ——————————————— **Date Prepared:**————————————

Scope Definition

Product scope is progressively elaborated from the project description and the product requirements in the Project Charter.

Project Deliverables

Project deliverables are progressively elaborated from the project description, the product characteristics and the product requirements in the Project Charter.

Project Acceptance Criteria

The criteria that needs to be met in order for a customer to accept a deliverable. Acceptance criteria can be developed for the entire project or for each component of the project.

Project Exclusion (Out of Scope)

Project exclusions clearly define what is considered out of scope for the project.

Project Constraints

Constraints that may be imposed on the project, such as a fixed budget, hard deliverable dates, or specific technology

Project Assumptions

Assumptions about deliverables, resources, estimates, and any other aspect of the project that the team holds to be true, real, or correct but has not validated.

Project Dependencies

Dependencies that exist due to other projects or initiatives.

Risk Management Plan

Project Title: ——————————————   Date Prepared: ——————————————

Methods and Approaches

Describe the methodology or approach to risk management. Provide information on how each of the risk management processes will be carried out, including whether quantitative risk analysis will be performed and under what circumstances.

Tools and Techniques

Describe the tools, such as a risk breakdown structure, and techniques, such as interviewing, Delphi technique, etc., that will be used for each process.

Roles and Responsibilities

Describe the roles and responsibilities for various risk management activities.

Risk Categories

Identify any categorization groups used to sort and organize risks. These can be used to sort risks on the risk register or for a risk breakdown structure, if one is used.

Definitions of Probability

Terms used to measure probability such as Very Low-Very High, or 01-1.0.	*Describe the ways of measuring probability: the difference between very high and high probability, etc. If using a numeric scale, identify the spread between bands of probability. (.05, .1, .2, .4, .8 or .2, .4, .6, .8).*

Definitions of Impact by Objective

Impact	*Scope*	*Quality*	*Schedule*	*Cost*
Specify terms used to measure impact, such as Very Low, Very High, or.01-1.0.	*Describe the ways of measuring impact on each objective. Objectives other than the ones listed here can be used. Define the difference between very high and high impact on an objective. If using a numeric scale, identify the spread between bands of impact (.05, .1, .2, .4, .8 or.2, .4, .6, .8). Note that the impacts on individual objectives may be different if one objective is more important than another.*			

Probability and Impact Matrix

This is a sample matrix for one project objective. The highlighting shows a balanced matrix that indicates ranking of High, Medium, or Low based on the probability and impact scores.

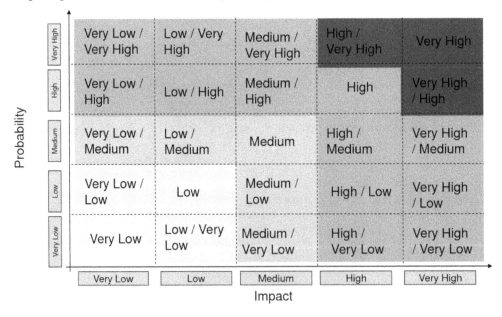

Risk Management Funding

Define the funding needed to perform the various risk management activities, such as utilizing expert advice or transferring risks to a third party.

Contingency Protocols

Describe the guidelines for establishing, measuring, and allocating both budget contingency and schedule contingency.

Frequency and Timing

Describe the frequency of conducting formal risk management activities and the timing of any specific activities.

Risk Audit Approach

Describe how often the risk management process will be audited, which aspects will be audited, and how discrepancies will be addressed.

ID	Description	P	L	E	First Indica-tor	Mitigation Ap-proach	Owner	Date Due
	\<List each major risk facing the project. Describe each risk in the form "condition – consequence". Example: "Subcontractor's staff does not have sufficient technical expertise, so their work is delayed for training and slowed by learning curve."\>	*P	*L	*E	\<For each risk, describe the earliest indica-tor or trigger condition that might indicate that the risk is turning into a problem.\>	\<For each risk, state one or more ap-proaches to avoid, transfer, control, minimize, or other-wise mitigate the risk. Accepting the risk is another option. Risk mitigation ap-proaches should yield demonstrable results, so you can measure whether the risk ex-posure is changing.\>	\<Assign each risk action to an indi-vidual.\>	\<State a date by which each mitigation action is to be com-pleted.\>

*P = Probability of occurrence of the risk, expressed as a number between 0.1 (highly unlikely) and 1 (guaranteed to happen). Alternatively, you could estimate this as Low, Medium, or High.

*L = Relative loss if the risk does turn into a problem, expressed as a number between 1 (mini-mal impact) and 10 (catastrophe). Alternatively, you could estimate this as Low, Medium, or High. Even better, estimate the actual loss in terms of calendar weeks for schedule impact, dollars for a cost impact, etc.

*E = Risk Exposure. If numeric values were assigned to Probability and Loss, then Risk Exposure = P * L. If relative values were used (Low, Medium, High), estimate the overall risk exposure using the following table:

Probability	Loss		
	Low	Medium	High
Low	Low	Low	Medium
Medium	Low	Medium	High
High	Medium	High	High

Once the risk exposures are calculated for each risk item, sort them in order of decreasing risk exposure. Focus mitigation efforts on items having the highest risk exposure

Stakeholder Analysis Matrix

Project Title:———————————————— **Date Prepared:** ————————————————

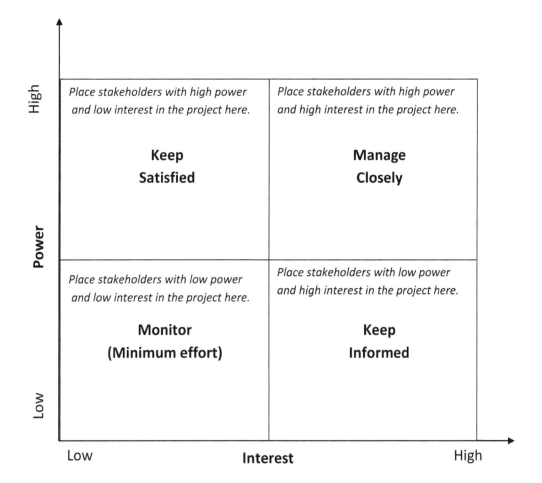

Keep
Satisfied

Manage
Closely

Monitor
(Minimum effort)

Keep
Informed

Stakeholders Management Strategy

Project Title:_____ **Date Prepared:** _____

Name	Influence	Impact Assessment	Strategies
Name of stakeholder	*Type of influence*	*Degree of influence or impact of influence*	*Strategies and tactics to maximize positive stakeholder influence and minimize or neutralize negative stakeholder influence.*

Stakeholder Register

Project Title: ———————————————— Date Prepared: ————————————————

Name	Position	Role	Contact Information	Requirements	Expectations	Influence	Classification

Business Requirements Document (BRD)

Organization
Name

Business
Requirements
Document

Project Name: _____

Version Number: _____

Prepared by: _____

Date: _____

Approved by:

Name, Department	Date
Name, Department	Date
Name, Department	Date

- Walk me through the BRD contents!
- What are the components of the BRD?
- How do you write a BRD?

BRD Table of Contents

Version Info

    Revision History

    RACI Matrix

    Peer Review

Business Case

Introduction

    Project overview

    Project goals and objectives

    Analysis performed to develop requirements

    Approach/Methodology

    Risks

    Assumptions

    Dependencies

Project Scope

    In-Scope

    Out-of-Scope

    Constraints

Business Processes and Work Flows

    Current process flow (As-Is)

    Future process flow (To-be)

    Gap Analysis

User Stories

    User story 1

    User story 2

Use Case

    Use case name

    Use case overview

    Actors

       Flow of events

       Special requirements

       Preconditions

       Post conditions

       Use case diagram

       Use case matrix

Requirements Matrix

       Business requirements

       Functional requirements

       User interface

       Training

       Security

       Other requirements

Success Criteria

References

Glossary

Version info

Revision History

It is the audit trail tracking revisions made to the document and the name of the person making the change.

Revision #	Date of Change	Change By	Description
0.1	*Mm/dd/yyyy*	*BA Name*	*Describe the change/update e.g. Added requirement #3* *Added assumption #2.2* *Removed dependency #4*

RACI Matrix

This section is to describe the roles played by the stakeholders/team members in the process of creating this BRD

R	Responsible	Usually the BA
A	Accountable	PM and BA
C	Consulted	Provides input (SME)
I	Informed	Approver or business SME

Name	Title	R	A	C	I

Peer Review

In some organizations, the BA is required to have a designated BA team peer member review the business requirements document prior to the Subject Matter Experts review/walkthrough to ensure the document meets the PMO best practices.

Revision #	Date	Name	Department

Business Case

This section answers the following questions:
- What is the purpose or justification of the project?
- What is the problem it will be solving?
- Why is it worth the investment?
- The rationale for why the project was selected above the other alternative solutions
- What are the project selection methods?
    - BCR – Benefit Cost Ration
    - EVA – Economic Value Added
    - IRR – Internal Rate of Return
    - PV – Present Value
    - NPV – Net Present Value
    - ROI – Return On Investment
    - Opportunity Cost
    - Payback Period

Note: some organizations add a business case section in the BRD. Later on in this chapter we will discuss details of the business case template

Introduction
Project overview
This section describes the project at a high level, and states that the business requirements document (BRD) is to document the needs of the business and end users, and to explain why these needs exist

Project goals and objectives

Describe the project business goals and objectives addressed by the customer.
Analysis performed to develop requirements

Describe how you created this BRD (e.g., business requirements were gathered with input from several business areas as part of the XXX project, including representatives from finance, human resources and actuarial areas)

Approach/Methodology

Describe the methodology used (waterfall, Rup, etc.)

Risks

List of anticipated risks to the implementation of these requirements
Assumptions

List of project assumptions that are being recommended to achieve the anticipated business outcomes, that if changed will impact the requirements in this document, such as:

- Project staff resources will be available as needed
- Required hardware resources will be available as needed
- There will be no change in regulations expected this year
- System XXX is retiring before the implementation of these requirements so it does not need to be updated
- Issues will be resolved in timely manner
- Outside consulting may be required for development work

Dependencies

In this section, describe the dependencies that exist due to other projects or initiatives, such as:
- A predecessor system should be updated for these requirements to work
- Waiting for an approval on one of the system's inputs
- The PMO is responsible for communicating all the changes to external vendors

Project Scope

Describe the project scope in details.

In Scope

Items, business areas and services that are considered in scope for the project:
1.
2.
3.
4.

Out-of-Scope

Items, business areas and services that are considered out of scope for the project:
1.
2.
3.
4.

Business Processes and Work Flows

This section illustrates the current (As-Is) and the future (To-Be) workflow for each business and system process impacted by the scope of the project.
- You can use any of the UML diagrams explained in chapter 5, depending on the project
- Swimlane (activity) diagram is most common
- Most organizations use Microsoft Visio to create UML Diagrams

Current process flow (As-Is)

How does the system currently work?

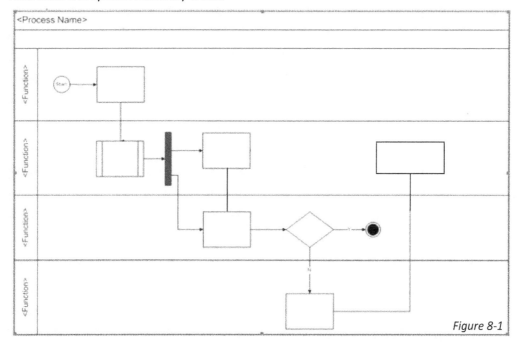

Figure 8-1

Future process flow (To-be)

What will the system look like after implementation of the requirements?

Gap Analysis

What is the difference between As-Is and To-Be states?

User Stories

This section describes in a narrative form how the end user or the customer would use the system. Tell the high level story for each requirement or set of requirements, as you find suitable. Here are some examples to help you get the feel of the user story:

User story 1 (Already a member)

Mary is a retail associate who is submitting a membership request for one of the clients she has recently met, Brian. Brian is already a member of the same retail shop but he does not know it. When Mary enters Brian's SSN, the system sends an error message informing her that Brian is already a member.

User story 2 (Print membership card)

Mary then wants to pull up Brian's information and print his membership card. She navigates to the shop website and enters her employee username and password on the right side of the home page. She will then click on the green print button below Brian's information.

Use Case

Use Case Name

Assign a unique name to your Use Case, preferably describing the functionality you want to present.

Overview

Write a brief description of the Use Case.

Actors

Any person, system or basically anything that interacts with the system causing it to respond to business events.

Actor/Role Name	Role Description	Objective
Actor 1	Briefly describe the role of the actor to the system and how the actor will use the system	What is the actor's goal? What does the actor need from the system? What is the expected outcome from the system?
Actor 2		
Actor 3		
Actor 4		
Actor 5		

Use case diagram

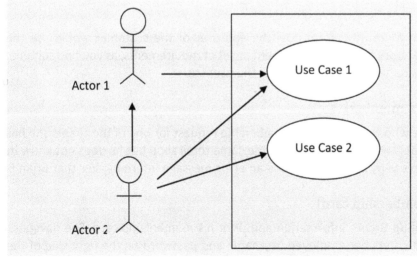

Figure 8-2

Flow of events

Use Case Name	<Assign unique Use Case name>
Use Case ID	< Assign unique Use Case ID>
Primary Actor	<Identify primary actor(s) that will initiate the use case>
Secondary Actor	OPTIONAL <Identify secondary actor(s) that may interact with the use case>
Brief Description	<Briefly describe the Use case scenario with expected result to meet the scenario goal>
Trigger	<Events or triggers that have to occur to fulfill the use case>
Pre-conditions	< Pre conditions that must be met and have direct dependency prior to initiating the use case>
Flow of Events	< Insert step-by-step flow of events that occur in the above use case. Add dependency within the flow of events, if any>
Post Conditions	< Insert success and error conditions for the use case>
Extension Point <error handling>	< This section includes information on IF there is secondary use case scenario OR the primary use case scenario fails, how does/should the application manage 'error handling'>
Quality Use case	IF APPLICABLE <Include quality requirements use case if applicable with measurable fit metrics>
Related Use Cases	< link to related use cases where it may have direct/indirect dependency.
Business Rules	< List application and mapped to steps in flow of events business rules here>

Requirements Matrix

Clearly insert the requirements stating their priority, business owner and status.

Business requirements

Business Require-ment	Requirement ID	Priority	Business Owner	Status
Insert the require-ment here	Unique ID for each req. to be used in success crite-ria table and RTM	Critical/important	Mark Steven-son (Actuarial dept.)	Draft
Create a log in field	SW10	Medium	Mark Steven-son (Actuarial dept.)	Reviewed
Create an error mes-sage that says (invalid username/password) when an incorrect password is entered	SW11	Low/Nice to have	Mark Steven-son (Actuarial dept.)	Approved
	SW12			Cancelled
				Need more info

Functional requirements

Same as the business requirements

User interface

Define exactly what the business wants the finished product to look and function like.

Security

Define the security measures that must apply to this product as defined by the business unit and the Security Policies and Procedures Guide.

Other requirements

Training

Describe any training needs due to the implementation of the new requirements; specify who is responsible for training, who needs to be trained, training schedule)

Training	Owner	Who will be trained?	Schedule
Training description	Who is responsible for providing the training?" Peng Sun (Training dept.)	Testing team	End of May 2014

Success Criteria

Accurately describe the success criteria for each requirement to be used by the testing team to ensure all requirements are implemented correctly.

Requirement ID	Success Criteria
SW10	When the member navigates to the company's website, a log in request appears on the right side of the home page
SW11	When the user enter incorrect username or password an error message appears saying (Invalid username or password)

References

List of all documents used as input to this BRD.

Glossary

Complete list of all terms, acronyms and abbreviations that are business or project-specific terms used in this BRD that might cause confusion to allow any external individual to properly interpret the document.

Term/Acronym	Definition
BRD	Business Requirement Document
SME	Subject Matter Expert

Inspection Checklist for Software Requirements

The following checklist should be completed after the initial requirements document is completed but before it is presented to the developers:

Organization and Completeness

- Are all internal cross-references to other requirements correct?
- Are all requirements written at a consistent and appropriate level of detail?
- Do the requirements provide an adequate basis for design?
- Is the implementation priority of each requirement included?
- Are all external hardware, software, and communication interfaces defined?
- Have algorithms intrinsic to the functional requirements been defined?
- Does the BRD include all of the known customer or system needs?
- Is any necessary information missing from a requirement? If so, is it identified as TBD?
- Is the expected behavior documented for all anticipated error conditions?

Correctness

- Do any requirements conflict with or duplicate other requirements?
- Is each requirement written in clear, concise, unambiguous language?
- Is each requirement verifiable by testing, demonstration, review, or analysis?
- Is each requirement in scope for the project?
- Is each requirement free from content and grammatical errors?
- Can all of the requirements be implemented within known constraints?
- Are any specified error messages unique and meaningful?

Quality Attributes

- Are all performance objectives properly specified?
- Are all security and safety considerations properly specified?
- Are other pertinent quality attribute goals explicitly documented and quantified, with the acceptable tradeoffs specified?

Special Issues

- Are all requirements actually requirements, not design or implementation solutions?
- Are the time-critical functions identified, and timing criteria specified for them?
- Have internationalization issues been adequately addressed?

Requirement Traceability Matrix (RTM)

Project Name: **Testing Manager:**
Project Manager: **Technical Developer Manager:**
Business Analyst:

Revision History

Revision #	Date of Change	Change By	Description
0.1	Mm/dd/yyyy	BA Name	

Business Requirement	Functional design	Use Case ID	Test Case Number
The requirement contained in the BRD	Contained in the FRD	Contained either within the BRD or a separate Use Case document	Contained in the test case document

- Consult with the technical design manager to complete the upstream mapping to one or more business requirement within the BRD.
- Consult with the test lead to obtain the test case number in the test scripts to map it to one or more business requirement within the BRD.
- The main goal of the RTM is to track the test cases back to the functional design back to the business requirements to ensure all the customer's requirements are implemented and tested.

- How do you ensure you accurately completed your RTM?
- I review the final RTM to make sure each requirement is uniquely and correctly identified and that each test case is traceable to a higher-level software functional and business requirement (e.g., system requirement, use case)

Use Case

Guidance for Use Case Template

Document each use case using the template shown in the Appendix. This section provides a description of each section in the use case template.

Use Case Identification

Use Case ID

Give each use case a unique integer sequence number identifier. Alternatively, use a hierarchical form: X.Y. Related use cases can be grouped in the hierarchy.

Use Case Name

State a concise, results-oriented name for the use case. These reflect the tasks the user needs to be able to accomplish using the system. Include an action verb and a noun. Some examples:
- View part number information.
- Manually mark hypertext source and establish link to target.
- Place an order for a CD with the updated software version.

Use Case History

Created By
Supply the name of the person who initially documented this use case.

Date Created
Enter the date on which the use case was initially documented.

Last Updated By
Supply the name of the person who performed the most recent update to the use case description.

Date Last Updated
Enter the date on which the use case was most recently updated.

Use Case Definition
Actors

An actor is a person or other entity external to the software system being specified who interacts with the system and performs use cases to accomplish tasks. Different actors often correspond to different user classes, or roles, identified from the customer community that will use the product. Name the actor that will be initiating this use case and any other actors who will participate in completing the use case.

Trigger
Identify the event that initiates the use case. This could be an external business event or system event that causes the use case to begin, or it could be the first step in the normal flow.

Description

Provide a brief description of the reason for and outcome of this use case, or a high-level description of the sequence of actions and the outcome of executing the use case.
Preconditions
List any activities that must take place, or any conditions that must be true, before the use case can be started. Number each precondition. Examples:

1. User's identity has been authenticated.

2. User's computer has sufficient free memory available to launch task.

Post-Conditions

Describe the state of the system at the conclusion of the use case execution. Number each post-condition. Examples:

1. Document contains only valid SGML tags.

2. Price of item in database has been updated with new value.

Normal Flow

Provide a detailed description of the user actions and system responses that will take place during execution of the use case under normal, expected conditions. This dialog sequence will ultimately lead to accomplishing the goal stated in the use case name and description. This description may be written as an answer to the hypothetical question, "How do I <accomplish the task stated in the use case name>?" This is best done as a numbered list of actions performed by the actor, alternating with responses provided by the system. The normal flow is numbered "X.0", where "X" is the Use Case ID.

Alternative Flows

Document other, legitimate usage scenarios that can take place within this use case separately in this section. State the alternative flow, and describe any differences in the sequence of steps that take place. Number each alternative flow in the form "X.Y", where "X" is the Use Case ID and Y is a sequence number for the alternative flow. For example, "5.3" would indicate the third alternative flow for use case number 5.

Exceptions

Describe any anticipated error conditions that could occur during execution of the use case, and define how the system is to respond to those conditions. Also, describe how the system is to respond if the use case execution fails for some unanticipated reason. If the use case results in a durable state change in a database or the outside world, state whether the change is rolled back, completed correctly, partially completed with a known state, or left in an undetermined state as a result of the exception. Number each alternative flow in the form "X.Y.E.Z", where "X" is the Use Case ID, Y indicates the normal (0) or alternative (>0) flow during which this exception could take place, "E" indicates an exception, and "Z" is a sequence number for the exceptions. For example "5.0.E.2" would indicate the second exception for the normal flow for use case number 5.

Includes

List any other use cases that are included ("called") by this use case. Common functionality that appears in multiple use cases can be split out into a separate use case that is included by the ones that need that common functionality.

Priority

Indicate the relative priority of implementing the functionality required to allow this use case to be executed. The priority scheme used must be the same as that used in the software requirements specification.

Frequency of Use

Estimate the number of times this use case will be performed by the actors per some appropriate unit of time.

Business Rules

List any business rules that influence this use case.

Special Requirements

Identify any additional requirements, such as nonfunctional requirements, for the use case that may need to be addressed during design or implementation. These may include performance requirements or other quality attributes.

Assumptions
List any assumptions that were made in the analysis that led to accepting this use case into the product description and writing the use case description.

Notes and Issues

List any additional comments about this use case or any remaining open issues or TBDs (To Be Determined) that must be resolved. Identify who will resolve each issue, the due date, and what the resolution ultimately is.

Use Case List

Primary Actor	Use Cases

Use Case - 001

Use Case ID:			
Use Case Name:			
Created By:		Last Updated By:	
Date Created:		Date Last Updated:	

Actors:	
Description:	
Trigger:	
Pre-conditions:	1.
Post conditions:	1.
Normal Flow:	1.
Alternative Flows:	
Exceptions:	
Includes:	
Priority:	
Frequency of Use:	
Business Rules:	
Special Requirements:	
Assumptions:	
Notes and Issues:	

Use Case - 002

Use Case ID:	
Use Case Name:	

Created By:		Last Updated By:	
Date Created:		Date Last Updated:	

Actors:	
Description:	
Trigger:	
Pre-conditions:	1.
Post conditions:	1.
Normal Flow:	1.
Alternative Flows:	
Exceptions:	
Includes:	
Priority:	
Frequency of Use:	
Business Rules:	
Special Requirements:	
Assumptions:	
Notes and Issues:	

Impact Assessment

ID	Functional Area	Impact (Y/N)	Impact Description	Impact Description	Impact Description	Processes Impacted	Processes Impacted	Processes Impacted	Level Of Confidence

Meeting Minutes

Project Title:	Date:
Time:	Reason:
Attendees:	

Meeting Objective:
Meeting Minutes Summary:

1. *Topic 1*
2. *Topic 2*
3. *Topic 3*

Actions and Next Steps	Assigned To	Due Date

Attendance Sheet

Date:

Meeting Objective:

NAME	DEPARTMENT

Summary/Comments:

RACI Matrix

Process description/name										
Process steps		**Department/area**						**Inputs**	**Outputs**	**Comments**
Artifact ID	**Artifact**	**Stakeholder 1**	**Stakeholder 2**	**Stakeholder 3**	**Stakeholder 4**	**Stakeholder 5**	**Stakeholder 6**			
1	Artifact 1	**C**	**C**	**A**						
2	Artifact 2		**R/A**	**A**						
3	Artifact 3		**R**		**R**					
4	Artifact 4		**I**	**R**	**A**					
5	Artifact 5			**I**						
6	Artifact 6									
7	Artifact 7									

RACI - Definition:
R = Responsible (Those who do the work to achieve the task)
A = Accountable (Those ultimately answerable for the correct and through completion of the deliverable, and the one who delegates the work to those responsible)
C = Consulted (Those whose opinions are sought, specially subject matter experts)
I = Informed (Those who are kept up-to-date on progress more often on the completion of the task)

Gap Analysis

Project Title: _____ **Date Prepared:**_____

Prepared by: _____ **For:** _____

Description: *(Explain why analysis is needed, what you are comparing, and other descriptive information)*

ID #	Current State	Future State	Gap Identification	Suggested Remediation
(Business unit, process, etc.)	*(Description of how things are now)*	*(Description of how things should be)*	*(Difference between Current and Future States)*	*(What needs to happen or change to go from how things are now to how things should be)*
Example: *Data sent to external customers*	*Data from ware-house is sent to systems solutions to be converted to format used by external customers*	*Functionality to convert formats is in system solutions' recent upgrade*	▪ *Retire Audit System before Jan 1 renewal* ▪ *Send data directly from data ware-house to external customers*	▪ *Modify feeds, tables, etc.* ▪ *Convert and load historical Audit System data into System Solutions* ▪ *Perform user testing with external customers*

Gap Analysis Diagram (Optional)

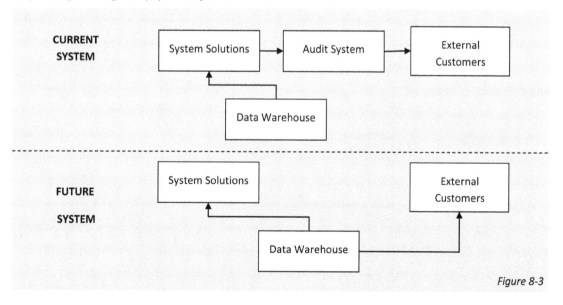

Figure 8-3

REFERENCES

Project Management Institute. (2009) Project Management Body Of Knowledge, Forth Edition.

Mulcahy, Rita (2011). PMP Exam Preparation, Seventh edition. RMC Publications.

International Institute of Business Analysis. (2006) A Guide to the Business Analysis Body of Knowledge. Version 1.6.

International Institute of Business Analysis. (2009) A Guide to the Business Analysis Body of Knowledge. Version 2.0.

Podeswa, H. (2008). The Business Analyst Handbook. Cengage Learning.

Womack, James P., Jones, T. Daniel. (2010) Lean Thinking. Free Press.

George, Michael L., Rowlands, David, Price, Mark, Maxey, John. (2004) The Lean Six Sigma Pocket Tool Book. McGraw-Hill.

OMG Unified Modeling Language (OMG UML), Superstructure. Object Management Group. Retrieved 2013-03-28. Version 2.4.1

www.ingramcontent.com/pod-product-compliance
Lightning Source LLC
Chambersburg PA
CBHW080402060326
40689CB00019B/4106